ASCOTT

BUCKINGHAMSHIRE

John Martin Robinson and others

SCALA

Ascott is half a mile east of Wing and 2 miles south-west of Leighton Buzzard, on the south side of the A418.

Chapters 1–3 and 6 have been written by John Martin Robinson; the essay on the pictures in Chapter 4 and the picture entries in Chapter 5 are by Karin Wolfe, on the basis of the entries in the 1963 catalogue by F. St. John Gore, with contributions by Alastair Laing; the essay on the ceramics and the ceramics entries are by Regina Krahl; the essay on the furniture and the remainder of Chapter 5 are by Tim Forrest; and Patrick Taylor gave assistance over Chapter 6.

The Publishers would like to thank Melanie Aspey, Geoffrey Bond, Alastair Laing and John Martin Robinson for their help in preparing this guide.

© Scala Publishers Ltd, 2008
Texts © the authors, 2008
Photography © Angelo Hornak/Sir Evelyn de Rothschild, 2008, except the following: pp. 7, 12 and 13 and figs. 1, 2, 4, 6, 7, 20, 23, 24, 29, 46, 66, 67, 68, 72, 111, 112, 130 © NTPL/ John Hammond, 2008; pp. 8–9 © RIBA, 2008; p. 61 © Harpur Garden Library, 2008; p. 62 © Garden Picture Library, 2008

First published in 2008 by
Scala Publishers Ltd
Northburgh House
10 Northburgh St
London EC1V 0AT
Tel: 020 7490 9900
www.scalapublishers.com

ISBN 10: 1 85759 504 1
ISBN 13: 9 78 1 85759 504 8

Project Editors: Esme West and Linda Schofeld
Design: Anikst Design, London
Printed and bound in Italy

10 9 8 7 6 5 4 3 2 1

British Library Cataloguing in Publication Data. A catalogue record for this book is available from the British Library.

CONTENTS

Introduction

'A palace-like cottage, the most luxurious and lovely thing I ever saw' was how William Gladstone's daughter, Mary, described Ascott after a visit in the 1880s. The man who created this combination of modesty and comfort was Leopold de Rothschild, from the third generation of the English branch of the great banking family, and his wife, Marie Perugia. Five branches of the de Rothschild family had settled in this part of Buckinghamshire in the mid-nineteenth century, combining the properties of Waddesdon Manor, Mentmore, Tring, Aston Clinton, Halton and Ascott over a 40,000 acre expanse. Ascott is the only one of the original de Rothschild houses in Buckinghamshire to still be the residence for descendants of its original occupant. The architect for Ascott was

George Devey, the pioneer of the 'Old English' Vernacular Revival, who progressively transformed and enlarged a simple farmhouse on the site from 1874. Devey's pupil James Williams carried on this work in the 1880s until Ascott had no fewer than 30 bedrooms.

In 1879 Leopold inherited part of the superb collection of his father, Baron Lionel de Rothschild, consisting primarily of Dutch and Flemish seventeenth-century cabinet pictures, but also of fine French eighteenth-century furniture. Although these were divided further among succeeding generations, Leopold and Marie, and their youngest son, Anthony, and his wife, Yvonne Cahen d'Anvers, added important paintings by Cuyp, Turner, Stubbs and Gainsborough so

far left
Ascott House from the south
terrace

left
Autumn colours on the north
lawn

that Ascott today contains one of the best small picture collections in Britain.

Anthony and Yvonne de Rothschild inherited the family fascination with collecting, and in the 1920s and 1930s acquired Chinese ceramics of the highest quality, in particular outstanding groups of Tang *sancai* ('three-colour') and turquoise- and purple-glazed Ming *fahua* ('cloisonné decoration') wares. In 1949, Anthony and Yvonne generously gave the Ascott Collection to the National Trust, together with the house, the grounds and an endowment.

Leopold and Marie de Rothschild were talented gardeners, who laid out the grounds of Ascott with a mixture of the formal and informal, including

exuberant Venus and Eros fountains by Thomas Waldo Story. Botanically, the garden was remarkable for its specimen trees and shrubs, many of which were chosen for their brilliant autumn colours. This variegated foliage remains a distinctive feature of the Ascott garden. Sir Evelyn, the only son of Anthony and Yvonne de Rothschild, and his wife, Lynn Forester, have continued the family commitment to the garden with the 2005 addition of 'Ascott Circle' by Richard Long and the creation of the Lynn Garden by Jacques and Peter Wirtz.

Chapter 1
The de Rothschild Family

Lord Stafford mines for coal and salt
The Duke of Norfolk deals in malt
Lord Douglas in red herrings
But noble name and miles of land
Palace, and park, and vassal band
Are pow'rless to the notes of hand,
Of *Rothschild* or the Barings.

The rise of the Rothschilds is one of the great success stories of the nineteenth century, and unique in that it encompassed nearly the whole European continent. Within 50 years of their emergence from the Frankfurt Ghetto in the late eighteenth century, the Rothschilds had established themselves as one of the leading banking dynasties and had been ennobled by the Habsburgs. Isaac Rothschild, a sixteenth-century ancestor, lived in the Judengasse in Frankfurt. His house had a red shield (*rotes schild*) hanging outside, and this was the origin of the family's resonant surname.

By the 1870s, the de Rothschilds owned no fewer than six estates within eight miles of Aylesbury. Their connection with the Vale of Aylesbury began soon after the death of Nathan de Rothschild (the founder of the London branch) in 1836. The Vale of Aylesbury was selected because it was considered a good hunting area, divided between several packs, including the Whaddon Chase, the Hertfordshire, the Old Berkeley and the South Oxfordshire. Moreover, it was easily accessible from London on the new railway from Euston to the north. At first the brothers hunted foxes, but they soon established their own staghounds to hunt deer. The deer, horses and hounds were kennelled in nearby Tring. A painting by Sir Francis Grant shows Lionel and his brothers Anthony, Nathaniel and Mayer hunting in the Vale in 1841. Fittingly this painting hangs today at Ascott (Lobby), which was developed pre-eminently as a hunting-lodge to serve the de Rothschild staghounds.

Ascott was constructed at the same time as Waddesdon Manor, but could not be more different. Rather than being a flamboyant continental château, it is a picturesque 'Old English' manor house of black and white half-timber, with red-tiled roofs and shafted brick chimneystacks. Of all the de Rothschild houses in the Vale of Aylesbury, it is the only one that looks as if it might have grown out of the Buckinghamshire clay, albeit a much enlarged and polished version of its particular type.

Above
Sir Francis Grant, PRA (1802–78)
Four Brothers of the de Rothschild
Family Following Hounds (see page 30)

Chapter 2
The Building of Ascott

Ascott, as it appears today, belies its age. Long, low and gabled, it looks like a heavily restored Tudor house. Its core is indeed an old farmhouse, thought to date from 1606. There seems little reason to doubt this, for, although the date inscribed inside the front porch is re-cut, it seems too specific to be made up and no doubt repeats a date discovered in the course of the Victorian alterations. The original farmhouse has undergone many changes. It was first moderately enlarged in 1874 to form 'Ascott Cottage', a pleasant country retreat, but was almost immediately expanded to make a fully fledged hunting-lodge with extensive stables, kennels and other outbuildings, before being again further enlarged to make a substantial Edwardian country house. In 1937–8, it was extensively remodelled when 37 rooms were removed to create the present appearance of an unassuming, rambling old manor house, the interior being almost wholly reconstructed at that time.

The Victorian enlargement of Ascott was begun in 1874 for Leopold de Rothschild after he acquired the property from his uncle, Baron Mayer, who owned the Ascott farmhouse as part of his nearby Mentmore property. Leopold employed as his architect one of the leading Victorian domestic practitioners, George Devey. Throughout Buckinghamshire, Devey had already designed several homes for the de Rothschild family, including a school and cottages at Aston Clinton for Anthony, stables and lodges at Mentmore for Mayer, and cottages at Halton for Alfred, who was Leopold's brother. Devey was responsible for all the subsequent alterations and additions to the house until his death in 1886, when the work was continued by his former partner, James Williams, and then by Williams's pupil, Walter Godfrey. The builder for the first phase of work at Ascott was John Durley of Bierton, who had also been employed else-where by various members of the de Rothschild family.

Unlike many Victorian architects, who were first and foremost designers of churches, Devey specialised in houses, and pioneered the revival of domestic vernac-ular styles: 'Queen Anne' in town and 'Old English' in

the country. His sensitivity towards building materials and his painterly eye for picturesque composition foreshadowed the work of Norman Shaw and Eden Nesfield and of the leading Arts and Crafts designers at the turn of the century, several of whom were his pupils. Devey himself was the nephew of the painter Augustus Egg and had been taught drawing by John Sell Cotman.

After Leopold de Rothschild's death in 1917, his widow, Marie, continued to live at Ascott. On her death in 1937, the house was inherited by their son Anthony and his wife, Yvonne, who immediately embarked on a complete reconstruction aimed at making the house easier to run and more in tune with the contemporary taste for simplicity. They demolished the stables, entrance arch and most of the service block, including James Williams's kitchen wing, dating from the 1880s. At the same time, much of the more fanciful Victorian detail was pared away, including the balustrade parapets and the loggias with their sgraffito decoration on the garden front, as well as several gables and bow windows. The marble basin from the forecourt and the elaborate topiary along the south front were likewise swept away.

The changes inside the house were even more drastic. The old dining room was removed. The former schoolroom and housekeeper's room were knocked together to make the present Dining Room. The site of the old farmhouse, latterly used as a library, was opened up and made into a large Inner Hall. The billiard room in the north wing was remodelled to make a new Library. At the same time almost all the Victorian fittings and decoration were stripped out. Moulded ceilings gave way to plain plaster. Dark carved oak was removed and replaced with lighter, simpler joinery. The large Jacobean and inglenook fireplaces gave way to simpler neo-Georgian designs. In all this Anthony and Yvonne de

Rothschild were motivated by the contemporary reaction against Victorian architecture and a desire to create a simple, muted background for the splendid collection they had assembled. The only fragment of the Devey interior decoration to survive was the frieze of the Common Room, inscribed with proverbs.

After his mother's death, Sir Evelyn assumed responsibility for Ascott and further remodelled and redecorated the interior. In 1988, the well-known Italian designer Renzo Mongiardino (who has also done much work for the French de Rothschilds in Paris, thus continuing the family tradition of employing the same designers) repainted the Dining Room walls in *trompe-l'oeil* to resemble blue-and-white Dutch tiles.

More recently, in 1997, Robert Kime remodelled the old drawing room as the current Porcelain Room, with specially designed Chinoiserie cases to display Anthony de Rothschild's collection. The Common Room was also remodelled under Kime's direction, and the four wooden door cases with entablatures were reinstated to George Devey's original design, based on old photographs, to complement the surviving proverbs frieze. This late twentieth-century decoration in the principal rooms has added a further dimension to the interest of Ascott.

far left
Ascott *c.*1878 with minimal alterations
to the original farmhouse

above left
The conservatory (begun 1879)
and part of the south front

above right
The arch connecting stables and offices
(begun 1878)

Chapter 3
Life at Ascott

The Leopold de Rothschilds entertained lavishly in all their houses: at 5 Hamilton Place in London, at Gunnersbury, at Newmarket and at Ascott. The Ascott season was essentially a winter one and ran from November to May; Gunnersbury, nearer to London, was used as the family's country house in the summer. This explains something of the character of the Victorian house at Ascott, with its rather dark, cosy rooms and the emphasis in the garden on topiary and multicoloured evergreens, which were just as effective in winter as in summer. Life at Ascott revolved around hunting and riding, but there was also a shoot, a golf course and skating on the Lily Pond to the north of the house. Guests encompassed political figures as well as many from the Prince of Wales's Marlborough House set. Regulars included the Marquess of Hartington (later 8th Duke of Devonshire) and his future wife, Louise, Duchess of Manchester, the Earl and Countess of Derby, Lord and Lady Farquhar, the Austrian minister Count Mensdorf, the Prime Minister A. J. Balfour and the Gosfords. Lord Gosford was a lord-in-waiting to the Prince of Wales and vice-chamberlain to Queen Alexandra. The Prince of Wales himself stayed at Ascott on several occasions. All these guests brought their own valets or maids to Ascott. Large extensions and alterations were made to Ascott in the 1880s to accommodate this periodic influx, as well as Ascott's own permanent staff, which included a groom of the chambers and several footmen in addition to the domestic and garden staff.

Their Victorian and Edwardian character unaltered, the ornate rooms, crammed with objects of all kinds, including much old oak furniture and Leo's collections of seventeenth-century continental silver and Fabergé, seemed very old-fashioned by 1937, when they were inherited by Anthony de Rothschild. He and Yvonne embarked on a total renovation, removing much of the house and many of its outbuildings, and remodelling the interior to create a series of lighter, simpler rooms, with modern central heating and bathrooms.

All this work was barely finished by the outbreak of the Second World War in 1939. Like many other English country houses, Ascott played a significant part in the war effort. The main house was used by the Chelsea Pensioners, who had been bombed out of the Infirmary at the Royal Hospital in London. The Cricket Pavilion was used to store 40 cases of objects evacuated from the London Museum as well as the principal treasures from the London synagogues, for which Anthony and Yvonne de Rothschild had offered a safe haven. All these objects survived the war and were returned to London once the threat of aerial bombardment had passed.

In 1949, Anthony and Yvonne de Rothschild gave the Ascott collection, together with the house, the

grounds of 261 acres and a generous endowment, to the National Trust. In handing over their art treasures to the nation, Anthony and Yvonne were continuing another de Rothschild tradition. Baron Ferdinand of Waddesdon Manor had bequeathed his collection of medieval and early Renaissance art to the British Museum in 1898, and Walter had left his zoology collection at Tring to the Natural History Museum in London. Baron Adolphe de Rothschild bequeathed a substantial art collection to the Louvre in 1900, and the children of Baron Edmond made an even more substantial donation of prints and drawings to it after his widow's death in 1936. Waddesdon Manor was also later bequeathed by his older son, James de Rothschild, to the National Trust. The aim at Ascott was that the collection would remain *in situ* in the house, with the family still in residence. The collection would thus be enjoyed by a wider public, but still in the 'appropriate surroundings of a beautifully furnished private house'.

After Anthony's death in 1961, Yvonne inherited Ascott, where she lived until her death in 1977. Ascott was inherited by their son, Sir Evelyn de Rothschild, who now lives at Ascott with his wife, Lynn Forester. Sir Evelyn and Lady de Rothschild use the house throughout the year, and have continued the original use of the house for entertaining family and friends. During recent years, Sir Evelyn and Lady de Rothschild have been hosts to members of the Royal Family, including HM Queen Elizabeth and HRH Prince Philip, as well as heads of state such as Prime Ministers Margaret Thatcher and Tony Blair and US President Bill Clinton.

left
Anthony and Yvonne de Rothschild

above
HM Queen Elizabeth and HRH Prince Philip with Sir Evelyn and Lady de Rothschild at Ascott

Chapter 4
The Collections

PICTURES

The pictures at Ascott reflect the passion for collecting of the de Rothschild family over three generations. The key figures are: Lionel de Rothschild, the eldest male of the second-generation English de Rothschilds; his youngest son and the builder of Ascott, Leopold; and his grandson Anthony, who gave the collection to the National Trust.

Lionel seems to have pursued works of art with the same steadfast determination he applied to his business affairs. He bought mainly seventeenth- and early eighteenth-century Dutch and Flemish cabinet pictures, which had first become popular with collectors in mid-eighteenth-century France, the period more usually associated with the *goût Rothschild*. These kinds of pictures soon also became popular among aristocratic British collectors, who competed eagerly for the many fine examples brought on to the market by the social upheavals of the French Revolution and Napoleonic Wars. They received the ultimate royal accolade in 1814, when the Prince Regent bought the superb Dutch and Flemish collection of another great banker, Sir Thomas Baring.

Lionel preferred to buy *en bloc* from well-known collections with a distinguished provenance. So, for instance, Hobbema's *Cottages in a Wood* (Common Room) came from the collection of Alexander Baring, Sir Thomas's younger brother, Adriaen van Ostade's superb *Peasants Carousing in Front of an Inn* (Dining Room) from the Van Loon collection in Amsterdam in 1878, and seven of the finest Dutch pictures now at Ascott, including the Van Mieris portraits in the Library, from the Heusch collection in London in 1854–7. Andrea del Sarto's *Madonna and Child with St John* (Porcelain Room), one of the masterpieces in the collection, came from the collection of George, Lord Vane, later 5th Marquess of Londonderry, in 1869.

Lionel bought glamorous full-length portraits of eighteenth-century beauties. The Gainsborough, said to

be of the Duchess of Richmond, (Library) and Reynolds's portrait of Mary Meyer (Hall Room) anticipated the fashion for such works later in the century among the American millionaires, catered for so successfully by the art dealer, Joseph Duveen.

Lionel also patronised contemporary artists, albeit in a modest way. A pair of paintings by Moritz Oppenheim (Hall Room), commemorating the founding of the de Rothschild banking fortune earlier in the century by Mayer Amschel, belong within the tradition of contemporary mid-Victorian historical genre painting, but also hang happily alongside Lionel's Dutch seventeenth-century cabinet pictures. In 1841, Lionel also sat for a portrait of himself riding to hounds with his three brothers in the Vale of Aylesbury (Lobby), which celebrated the arrival of the second generation of the English de Roth-schilds in Buckinghamshire. Lionel chose the fashionable painter of the moment, Francis Grant, who had made his reputation the previous year with a portrait of Queen Victoria and Lord Melbourne at Windsor.

On his death in 1879, Lionel's three sons each inherited one-third of his collection of pictures. Ascott, therefore, preserves only a small fragment of the pictures he assembled. His son Leopold seems to have been more interested in acquiring racing trophies than paintings. It is also unlikely that many of the more important works he inherited were hung at Ascott, as it was used for such comparatively brief periods of the year and he had other substantial houses at Hamilton Place in London, Newmarket and Gunnersbury. Leopold did, however, buy, from the Demidoff sale in 1870, the four Boucher tondi of *The Arts* (Library Passage), which are so typical of de Rothschild taste. The Stubbs *Five Brood Mares* (Hall Room) is also a worthy testament to Leopold's love of horses.

It was Anthony and Yvonne de Rothschild who installed Lionel's pictures at Ascott (or at least that portion which Anthony inherited), and they were largely responsible for the way the collection is hung today – informally, in a comfortable domestic setting. Although his principal interest as a collector was in Chinese ceramics (see below), Anthony made several major additions to the picture collection, including Cuyp's *View of Dordrecht* (Dining Room), Gainsborough's *The Hon. Thomas Needham* (Hall Room) and Turner's *Cicero at his Villa*. One more Stubbs came to Ascott in 1926, as a wedding present from Anthony's cousin, James de Rothschild. There are now three works by Stubbs in the house – appropriate decoration for what was once a hunting-box.

In 1931, Anthony also inherited Italian paintings from his father's cousin Constance, Lady Battersea, whose husband was an enthusiastic patron of Victorian painters and had a passion for all things Italian: 'When common sense, in the shape of his wife,' as she put it,

far left
Meindert Hobbema
(1638–1709)
Cottages in a Wood (see page 34)

above
Andrea del Sarto (1486–1531)
The Madonna and Child with St John (see page 38)

'made him turn his back on the attractions of Italy, he did his best at any costs to transplant Italian colouring and Italian designs into his London and Norfolk homes.' The best of these include the Tiepolo tondo (Library), which had belonged to one of the greatest of all Tiepolo collectors, Edward Cheney.

Anthony and Yvonne also employed the services of contemporary artists. Specifically, from 1920 to 1928, Alfred Munnings took residence at Ascott at various times. He painted up to 19 pictures for Anthony de Rothschild during those years. Six remain in the private collection of Sir Evelyn and Lady de Rothschild, but 13 were destroyed during the Second World War when the warehouse of Christies, where they had been stored for safekeeping, was bombed. About his time at Ascott, Munnings wrote in his autobiography: 'Later a bomb fell, and Christie's was completely destroyed. So ended my labours at the Southcourt Stud. After the war Mr. Anthony de Rothschild told me what had happened when I met him at Ascott. This was the hardest blow I had ever known. Never did an artist have a finer chance than this to paint what he would wish. Not only did the patron say, "Paint whatever you like, just whatever you feel inclined to do," but he afterwards paid for everything at my figure. I recollect going to see him at the bank, New Court, St. Swithin's Lane, to be given the largest and most generous cheque I had so far received for my work.'

Sir Evelyn and Lady de Rothschild have continued the tradition of bringing contemporary artists to live and work at Ascott. They commissioned the renovation of the former gas house, built by Leopold as one of Britain's first private power facilities, into an artist's studio. Mark Alexander was the first artist to occupy the space. Alexander (b. 1966, England) received his BFA from Oxford University in 1996. Alexander's style is characterised by meticulous labour-intensive brushwork. His art often reinvents the icons of the past, including the Shield of Achillies and Van Gogh's portrait of Paul Gachet. Alexander's painstaking technique, requiring many months to complete a single work, has attracted both praise and befuddlement from critics. Alexander cuts an enigmatic figure in the art world, attracting the interest of some of its most influential collectors. From 1993, when his career began, until 2008 he produced only 22 paintings. This is due to a sort of manic fastidiousness. The works combine elements of eighteenth-century classicism, nineteenth-century photography and modern photo-realism.

CERAMICS

The collection of Chinese ceramics at Ascott was formed by Anthony de Rothschild, mainly during the 1920s and 1930s. His interest in this subject may have been kindled by a trip around the world in 1910 and encouraged by the vogue for collecting Chinese wares in the following decades, particularly in Britain and France. The collection partly reflects the fashion of the time, but it also includes many pieces then only appreciated by a small group of connoisseurs.

Anthony appears to have been fascinated in particular by the Chinese potters' ability – throughout history – to achieve glazes in vivid colours, ranging from yellow and green through blue to turquoise and purple. The collection thus includes early glazed pottery from the Han (206 BC–AD 220), Tang (AD 618–907) and Liao (907–1125) dynasties. The remarkable group of Tang dynasty wares includes, among several *sancai* ('three-colour' – i.e., green, yellow and brown) examples, a large monochrome blue-glazed grain jar and cover, which is one of the finest Tang dynasty pottery vessels in existence.

Among the stonewares of the Song (960–1279), Jin (1115–1234) and Yuan (1279–1368) dynasties, the most remarkable group are the Jun wares of Henan province

that few examples are preserved in China today. These bright, mainly turquoise and purple-glazed ceramics dating from the mid- to late Ming dynasty (1368–1644), largely made in south China (Jingdezhen, in Jiangxi province), represent practical utensils originally intended for use on temple or house altars, or out of doors. Anthony de Rothschild assembled what today is probably the most representative collection of such wares in the world. The term *fahua* ('cloisonné decoration'), originally denoting a type of ware where raised lines of slip separate the different glaze colours – similar to the way metal wires keep apart the enamels on cloisonné wares – soon became synonymous with the characteristic colour scheme of such wares: turquoise, blue and purple.

The turquoise-glazed porcelains of the Ming, and particularly the Qing dynasty (1644–1911) were very popular in France, and many examples seen at Ascott came from the family of Anthony's wife, Yvonne Cahen d'Anvers. They harmonise so perfectly with his own collecting interests, however, that they are not recognisable in the house as a distinct group.

While most of the earlier ceramics came to Europe as antiques, the porcelains of the Kangxi period (1662–1722) in the Qing dynasty were sent straight from the kilns to the south Chinese ports, to be shipped to Europe. Those painted in the colours of the *famille verte*, which are most characteristic of this period, have been ubiquitous in English country houses ever since the early eighteenth century. Here, too, Anthony de Rothschild picked some unusually fine and large examples, which are rarely seen elsewhere.

FURNITURE

The furniture is a mixture of eighteenth-century English and French pieces. Leopold de Rothschild inherited the French ones from his father, Lionel, from Gunnersbury Park. The English portion was collected by Anthony and Yvonne de Rothschild. The makers of the French furniture are well documented, unlike the English makers. This is because in eighteenth-century France there was a strict guild system which obliged every member, once accepted, to stamp his work. In England, definite attributions can only be made where original designs or bills still exist.

Among the delights of the English collection are the three suites of chairs and sofas dating from the middle of the eighteenth century. They are upholstered in two cases

in north China. They are characterised by simple shapes and an absence of decoration, but also by their striking milky lavender and purple glazes, which were often used in highly effective combinations.

Anthony de Rothschild kept most of the invoices for his purchases, which he made mainly through London and Paris dealers. They clearly show that these early ceramics, which were then not very fashionable, were mostly relatively inexpensive. They were of interest mainly to specialists and enthusiasts such as the members of the Oriental Ceramic Society, to whose exhibitions he regularly lent. Only the comprehensive exhibition of Chinese art held at the Royal Academy in London in 1935–6 made them known to a wider audience. This exhibition included 14 of Anthony de Rothschild's Chinese pieces.

Much more popular in Europe in the early decades of this century were the so-called *fahua* wares – so much so

left
Jar and cover, Tang dynasty
(see page 41)

above
Two vases, on tripod pedestals,
Qing dynasty (see page 39)

with wonderful contemporary needlework covers in both *gros* and *petit point* and in the third case with Mortlake tapestry. Throughout the house are fine examples of the English cabinetmaker's art. The collection ranges onwards from the early years of the eighteenth century, and there are good examples of most types of cabinet work. In the Hall Room is a mahogany side-table that dates from the mid-1750s and which is of a style known as 'Irish Chippendale'. The term is used to denote furniture of this period made in Ireland and influenced by the designs of Thomas Chippendale and his contemporaries. What they may have lacked in precision of composition was made up for by the vigour of the carved decoration. An interesting pair of console tables also found in the Hall Room is in the style of William Kent, *c*.1740. Demi-octagonal in shape, they have green marble tops, and the carving displays the usual Kentian motifs of swags, lion masks and hairy paw feet. Originally they would probably have been decorated in paint and parcel gilt, but they are now in stripped pine. The Common Room contains a good pair of Queen Anne gesso mirrors, which have a central shell as decoration to their shaped tops. Displayed throughout the house are some good examples of Queen Anne stools and George I chairs.

The French furniture exemplified the family's favourite form of interior decoration. Particularly interesting is the secretaire in the Porcelain Room, which is ebonised with wonderful panels of Japanese lacquer framed with ormolu mounts. Its fall-front opens to reveal an interior fitted with drawers and a central recess inlaid with panels of marquetry depicting flowers. It is stamped 'BVRB JME', denoting the *ébéniste* Bernard van Risenburgh, who was of Flemish origin but is regarded as one of the foremost craftsmen of French eighteenth-century furniture; another stamp, '+JOSEPH+', possibly indicates that Joseph Baumhauer (d.1772) repaired the piece at a later date.

Many other famous names of the period are represented, including Claude-Charles Saunier (1735–1807), Philippe-Claude Montigny (1734–1800), F. Rubestuck (1722–85), Adam Weisweiler (1740–1820) and Roger Vandercruse, known as Lacroix (RVLC) (1728–99). The great Jean-Henri Riesener (1734–1806) made the parquetry *bureau à cylindre* in the Lobby, which bears his stamp. Riesener succeeded Gilles Joubert as *ébéniste du roi* in 1774 and provided much furniture for Louis XV and XVI. One piece that has a royal provenance is the splendid Transitional commode by Mathieu-Guillaume Cramer (active 1771–94), which is in the Common Room. Cramer worked

as a subcontractor to Joubert, and it is known that this commode was one of a pair costing 4,720 *livres* supplied for the bedroom of the Comtesse de Provence, the sister-in-law of Louis XVI, at Fontainebleau.

An interesting early example of Louis XVI revival furniture is the small tricoteuse (work-table) in the Common Room, which is set with small Sèvres plaques and dates from the reign of Louis XVIII (1815–24).

left
Louis XV black lacquer
fall-front secretaire stamped
Bernard van Risenburgh *c.1760*
(see page 39)

right
French ormolu-mounted tricoteuse,
first half 19th century (see page 37)

Chapter 5
Tour of the House

All pictures are in oils on canvas, unless otherwise stated. Only the more important pieces of Chinese ceramics are mentioned, as full lists are available in each room. Only the more important pieces of furniture are included.

THE OUTER HALL

If you turn round and look up as you enter the front door, you will see a piece of exposed beam carved with the date 1606. Although a drawing surviving among Devey's plans for the house suggests that it was re-cut in the nineteenth century, this may record a date discovered during the dismantling of the earlier, seventeenth-century house.

The frame scroll records the wartime residence at Ascott of the Chelsea Pensioners from 1941 to 1947, after the bombing of the Infirmary of the Royal Hospital. They occupied all the ground-floor rooms, apart from the Library.

1

THE HALL ROOM

PICTURES

1 MORITZ DANIEL OPPENHEIM (1800–82)
The Elector of Hesse Entrusting Mayer Amschel Rothschild
with his Treasure
Mayer Amschel Returning the Inventory of the Elector of
Hesse, Who Refuses It
The two paintings together illustrate the well-known
story of how the founder of the de Rothschild bank,
Mayer Amschel de Rothschild, not only saved the
treasure of Elector William I from falling into the hands
of Napoleon but was also, through a series of shrewd
investments abroad, able to win the confidence of the
Elector and remain his banker. Oppenheim was so
closely associated with the family that he was known as
'the painter of the Rothschilds, and the Rothschild of
painters'.

2 SIR JOSHUA REYNOLDS, PRA (1723–92)
Miss Meyer as Hebe
Mary Meyer sat to Reynolds ten times between August
1771 and January 1772. Her father, Jeremiah Meyer, was
the foremost miniaturist of his time, and, as no pay-
ments are recorded for this portrait, it may have been
painted in exchange for work presented to Reynolds.
Mary Meyer was said to have been ill tempered and to

2

3

4

have attempted to run away from home, although here Reynolds portrays her, in the classicising guise of Hebe serving nectar to Jupiter, as docile and enchanting.

3 THOMAS GAINSBOROUGH, RA (1727–88)
The Hon. Thomas Needham (d. 1773)
The eldest son of the 10th Viscount Kilmorey, in the uniform of the 3rd Footguards. The steel throat-piece, known as a 'gorget' (a vestige of medieval armour), was worn by officers until 1830. The young man holds a 'spontoon' (a weapon carried by infantry officers until 1796), yet both his hands are concealed. Although Gainsborough often painted sitters with their hands tucked under their waistcoats, in this instance it seems a curious pose. Needham's father was also painted by Gainsborough (Tate Britain) at the time of his succession in 1768, the approximate date of the present picture.

4 WILLIAM HOGARTH (1697–1764)
Miss Woodley
Once wrongly thought to be of Jane Hogarth, the artist's wife (the actual portrait of whom is in a private collection). R. B. Beckett suggests this may be the portrait of Miss Woodley once in the collections of Benjamin West, H. R. Willet and Baron Leopold de Rothschild. She married Vaughan, the comedian. Laurence Gowing dates the picture to *c.*1738.

5 ATTRIBUTED TO SIR MARTIN ARCHER SHEE, PRA (1769–1850)
Miss Kelly
Previously attributed to Hoppner, but typical of Archer Shee's accomplished portraiture of the 1790s. The provenance of the portrait has traditionally been Irish, which further strengthens the attribution to Shee, who was born outside Dublin and spent his early years at the

6

Royal Dublin Society Schools, before going on to the Royal Academy in London. A version in America has customarily been ascribed to Archer Shee.

6 GEORGE STUBBS, ARA (1724–1806)

Five Brood Mares at the Duke of Cumberland's Stud Farm in Windsor Great Park, Signed

Stubbs was painting similar pictures of mares and foals, probably his most beautiful and original works, during the 1760s and early 1770s. Basil Taylor first pointed out that this is the sole extant painting in which mares appear without foals, and that it can thus be identified with the *Brood Mares* exhibited at the Society of Artists in 1765. According to a note made by Horace Walpole in his copy of the catalogue of the exhibition, it belonged to the Duke of Cumberland. The setting is therefore Windsor Great Park, where the Duke had his stud farm.

7 GEORGE ROMNEY (1734–1802)

Sarah Ley, Mrs Tickell

Sarah Ley was a 'beautiful girl of eighteen' when she married the dramatist Richard Tickell in 1789. She had sat to Romney no fewer than 23 times before her marriage and did so again 14 times afterwards. Sittings for this picture took place in 1791–2. The subject was celebrated in the newspapers of the day: 'Romney's Portrait of Mrs Tickell is an exquisite display of graceful outline. To the fair subject of this Picture the Prologue of *The Fugitive* is indebted for four conclusive verses . . . and the sincerity of Mr Tickell's Inspiration will not be questioned when the beauty and accomplishments of the Lady are consulted.' Despite the fame of *The Fugitive* and of his staging of the opera *The Carnival of Venice*, Richard Tickell (who was the brother-in-law of Richard Brinsley Sheridan by his first marriage) could not maintain his

7

13

luxurious way of life and fell deeply into debt. After he committed suicide in 1793, his young wife, who 'had a small dowry and expensive tastes', was criticised as being 'without mind in her countenance or anything else'. The picture may have been cut down at some time, as the feathers on the hat are not all visible at the top.

FURNITURE

8 A George III mahogany serpentine dressing chest with carved foliage and parcel gilt, *c.*1775.

9 An Irish mid-Georgian mahogany side-table with a frieze of scallop shells and scrolling foliage, and cabriole legs with paw feet, *c.*1750.

10 A Louis XV ormolu-mounted kingwood and tulipwood *bureau plat*, *c.*1750

11 *Either side of the fireplace* is a pair of William Kent-style stripped pine side-tables of demi-octagonal shape with green marble tops, nineteenth century.

12 *Around the room* is a fine set of five George II mahogany armchairs, *c.*1750, attributed to Giles Grendey, with shaped arms and cabriole legs terminating in eagle claw-and-ball feet. The contemporary needlework covers in *gros* and *petit point* show ladies and gentlemen in garden landscapes, animals and flowering plants.

TEXTILES

13 Two early eighteenth-century needlework panels on canvas. The wool and silk needlework is of sprays of flowers and butterflies.

15

14 A pair of Sèvres pot-pourri vases (1760) with ormolu mounts, *c.*1780.

15 A pair of Meissen leopards on Louis XV ormolu bases.

16 *Below the paintings by Hogarth and Shee* are two turquoise *fahua* wine jars *c.*1500, one painted with the Four Scholarly Accomplishments (painting, writing, music and chess), the other with the God of Longevity and the Eight Immortals.

17 The contemporary jar *below the painting by Romney* is the remaining lower half of a massive vase in the shape of a bottle gourd.

THE DINING ROOM

Devey's dining room was removed during Anthony and Yvonne de Rothschild's remodelling of Ascott in the late 1930s. At the same time this new room was created out of the former schoolroom and housekeeper's room. The walls were painted by Renzo Mongiardino with *trompe-l'oeil* blue-and-white Delft tiles in imitation of the dados found in seventeenth-century Dutch interiors. The carved wood fireplace is in the early eighteenth-century style.

PICTURES

18 NICOLAES BERCHEM (1620–83)
Herdsmen and Animals in a Landscape, Signed
Dating to the late 1650s, this sunlit pastoral idyll is characteristic of Berchem's romanticising Italianate phase.

19 NICOLAES BERCHEM (1620–83)
Cattle and Sheep in a Landscape, Panel, Signed and dated 1655
Typical of the kind of small pastoral genre picture that Berchem produced in great quantity: more than 800 paintings are now ascribed to him, many of which were also reproduced in engraved form.

20 PHILIPS WOUWERMAN (1619–68)
A Winter Landscape, Panel
Winter landscapes are rare in Wouwerman's *oeuvre* and thus difficult to date. The artist comments on the transience of life by contrasting the lively activity of the skaters with the barrenness of the frozen landscape.

21 ADRIAEN VAN OSTADE (1610–85)
The Interior of an Inn with Peasants Playing Cards, Panel, Signed and dated 1674
The disorder inside this shabby inn is meant to underline the patrons' degenerate way of life. Smoking, drinking and gambling were all vices antithetical to seventeenth-century Dutch notions of social order, and van Ostade's picture gently underlines the danger of moral decay.

22 ANTHONIE VERSTRALEN (c.1593–1641)
A Winter Landscape, Panel, Monogrammed and dated 1641
Verstralen, or Van Stralen, painted in the manner of Hendrick Avercamp, a specialist in winter landscapes. The scene depicts a bustling thoroughfare, the frozen river serving the painter as a stage set on which his play

20

takes place. The old man in a fur hat in the foreground personifies winter.

23 ISAACK VAN OSTADE (1621–49)

A Village Fair, Panel, Indistinctly signed and dated 1649
Isaack was the younger brother and pupil of Adriaen van Ostade. *A Village Fair* demonstrates his particular talent for large-scale outdoor scenes, combining popular genre with landscape. Here the main road of the village is used as a stage on which the local fair unfolds. Tall trees punctuate the route, lending a touch of colour to the drab houses they frame. Each figure is carefully characterised, from the woman balancing a basket on her head, keys hanging down from her waist, to the unruly children gathered around the cider-maker and the lovers embracing on the left.

24 ADRIAEN VAN OSTADE (1610–85)

Peasants Carousing in Front of an Inn, Signed and dated 1670 or 1679
This raucous scene of peasant life points up the seventeenth-century Dutch preoccupation with moral rectitude. Dissolute adults set a poor example for their children; indeed the boy sitting spellbound in the foreground has been left to his own devices. The ramshackle inn, of simple daub and brick, is overgrown with vines, the broken windows demonstrating real, as well as moral, decay. In contrast, the tall spire of the church, just visible in the background, beckons the morally upright.

25 ADRIAEN VAN OSTADE (1610–85)

The News, Panel (oval), Signed and dated 1650
Van Ostade's talent was not confined to scenes of large gatherings, as this small yet picturesque panel illustrates. The three elderly figures, grouped together in the common social pursuits of drinking, pipe-smoking and news-reading, allow us a glimpse of Dutch low life, a subject that so appealed to contemporary collectors.

26 JAN STEEN (1626–79)

Itinerant Musicians, Panel, Signed and dated 1659
Jan Steen's paintings almost always contained moral admonitions, which would have been understood by his Dutch seventeenth-century audience. The setting is rigorously defined by an arch, which, along with the steps and iron balustrade, separates the upright middle-class household from the disorder and perceived degeneracy of street life. Steen also alludes to the sensory

23

24

temptations posed by music and the danger of its corrupting the young.

27 PHILIPS WOUWERMAN (1619–68)
A Hawking Party Setting Out, Monogrammed
The Italianate landscape of overgrown ruins with classical buildings in the distant background suggests a late date of at least 1660.

28 MANNER OF JAN HACKAERT (1628–AFTER 1685?)
A Wooded Landscape, Signed
Despite being commissioned as a topographical draughtsman, almost all of Hackaert's painted landscapes appear to be of imaginary views. This wooded scene is of a type the artist pioneered, with tall trees dominating the landscape and either a road or river leading the eye abruptly back. Although close to Hackaert's style and inscribed with the artist's name, this picture is not up to his normal standard. The figures are particularly weak and cannot be attributed to Hackaert's usual collaborators, Adriaen van der Velde, Nicolaes Berchem or Johannes Lingelbach.

29 AELBERT CUYP (1620–91)
View of Dordrecht
Dordrecht is seen from the north-east, the point of conjunction of the two rivers, the Oude Maas and Dordtse Kil,

marked by the 'Standaard-Molen' windmill. A two-masted merchant ship flying Dutch flags is anchored outside the town, while smaller transport ships (*kaags*) sail slowly in fading early afternoon light. The massive square tower is the Grote Kerk, dating from the late fourteenth and early fifteenth centuries, one of the grandest of Dutch churches; the attenuated clock tower on the left belongs to the Town Hall. The quayside is shown as it was rebuilt in 1647, but the picture itself is generally dated later, to the early or mid-1650s. By this time the Netherlands was at peace, following the end of the Thirty Years War in 1648, so there is none of the wealth of warships shown in Cuyp's earlier views of shipping on the Maas. Instead the raft is an allusion to the hardwoods shipped down from Germany on which Dordrecht's prosperity had been based.

Strangely, for a painting of this consequence, we have no record of who owned it before it was reputedly imported into England by Captain William Baillie, who sundered it into two pictures serving as pendants, called 'Morning' and 'Evening', before selling it. The first certain record of them is in Sir George Colebrooke's sale in 1774. It is also singular that it bears no trace of any signature, yet has not been cut down. These points may all indicate that Cuyp painted the picture for his own pleasure and use, very possibly around the time of his marriage in 1658 to the wealthy Cornelia Bosman, after which he painted less and less.

29

Ever since it was reunited *c*.1841–2, this picture has been reckoned one of Cuyp's supreme achievements, if not his outright masterpiece.

30 AELBERT CUYP (1620–91)
A Landscape with a Horseman on a Road, Panel, Signed
This fine landscape, showing the ruined castle of Ubbergen, was not discussed by Reiss in his 1975 catalogue raisonné, but is listed in the traditional sources and must be considered autograph. The delicate early morning sunlight that strikes the figures is inimitable.

FURNITURE

31 *Below the Cuyp at the far end of the room* is an early George III mahogany serving-table in the manner of John Cobb, *c*.1765. It has six scrolling acanthus-carved legs and a frieze decorated with classical urns, husks, ribbons and *paterae*.

32 *Below two tables* are two George II mahogany wine coolers of oval gadrooned form, *c*.1740.

33 *In the bay window* is a William and Mary gateleg table with an oval top, *c*.1700.

34 *In the centre of the room* is a walnut gateleg dining-table in four sections (two are arranged along the inside wall), late nineteenth or early twentieth century.

35 *Round the dining-table* is a set of mid-Georgian-style early twentieth-century dining-chairs covered in hide upholstery.

METALWORK

36 Silver-plated wall sconces with the de Rothschild device of shield and five arrows originally designed by Walter Godfrey for the former Drawing Room.

TEXTILES

37 Mid-eighteenth-century Kirmanshah carpet, lobed blue medallion, with iron red border.

CERAMICS

38 *On the table by the window* is a massive Chinese porcelain dish with ladies in a garden playing a pitch-pot game, painted in colours of the *famille verte* and gilding. It is one of the largest dishes of the Kangxi period (1662–1722).

39 *On a side-table* are two large blue-and-white jars, the ovoid one dating from the late Ming period (1368–1644), the octagonal one from the Kangxi reign.

THE LOBBY

The bay to the right as you enter was the original front door to the house. This small space is hung with British sporting paintings.

PICTURES

40 JOHN FREDERICK HERRING THE ELDER (1795–1865)

Memnon

Herring was one of the greatest Victorian horse and animal painters. He is perhaps most famous for his portraits of the Derby and St Leger winners, of which he painted 21 and 33 consecutive examples respectively. Although he began modestly as a coach-driver and coach-painter, he gained great recognition in his lifetime.

Memnon, foaled in 1822 by Whisker out of Manuella, won the Champagne Stakes at Doncaster as a two-year-old. In 1825, again at Doncaster, he won the St Leger and was immortalised immediately after the race by Herring. The 1825 St Leger was the first race to have its result reported to London by carrier pigeon.

41 GEORGE STUBBS, ARA (1724–1806)

Two Horses in a Paddock, Panel, Signed and dated 1788

Although the picture is recorded as having been commissioned by John Hanson, who is said to have been thought mad to pay 80 guineas for it, the setting may well be the famous stud farm of Lord Grosvenor. The fences and building seen in the background between the two horses match the setting of the *Mares and Foals beneath Large Oak Trees* (collection of Anne, Duchess of Westminster), which was ordered by Lord Grosvenor. Grosvenor often gave his horses botanical names, and Stubbs would allude to this caprice by painting the appropriate species in the foreground. Broad-leaved plants are depicted in the right foreground of the Ascott picture – an indication perhaps of the horses' names. The painting is in fine condition and shows the great abstraction of composition of which Stubbs was capable. The two horses face one another in a frieze-like arrangement of startling originality.

42 GEORGE STUBBS, ARA (1724–1806)
Pumpkin, Panel, Signed and dated 1773

Pumpkin (1769), by Match'em out of Old Squirt Mare, was bred by the jockey John Pratt and owned jointly by the politician Charles James Fox and the Hon. Thomas Foley (later Lord Foley). He was first raced in 1772, went on to win 16 out of his 24 races and was painted several times by Stubbs. The jockey up is Old South, the most celebrated of the day, and Pumpkin is shown at a gap in the Ditch Mound, Newmarket.

43 CHARLES TOWNE (1763–1840)
Felt

Towne was famous for his portraits of horses set in fine landscapes, but he first gained notoriety for copying Stubbs's work. Stubbs objected to the Royal Academy, which recommended that Towne's copies be destroyed. The pictures were, however, not destroyed, and Towne continued to receive important commissions.

44 H. CALOW (?)
Flying Kate, Signed and dated 1832

No artist of this name is identifiable, and one should ask whether the signature has not been tampered with, garbling that of such a well-known horse painter as H. B. Chalon (1770–1849). The town pictured in the background may be York (the Minster seems just visible).

45 JOHN BEST (ACTIVE 1750–1801)
Gimcrack

Gimcrack, foaled in 1760 by Cripple, the Godolphin Arabian's son, out of a Partner mare, was one of the best-known eighteenth-century racehorses. His greatest victory was in 1765, when he raced against Sir James Lowther's Ascham in a 1,000 guineas match at Newmarket. Betting is said to have exceeded £100,000 and

46

Gimcrack's owner, the 2nd Viscount Bolingbroke, commissioned Stubbs to portray Gimcrack winning the race. Gimcrack was later sold to Lord Grosvenor, for whom he won the Whip at Newmarket in 1770.

46 AFTER WILLIAM HOGARTH (1697–1764)
A Harlot's Progress: Quarrels with her Protector

A copy of the second episode of *A Harlot's Progress.* The series was engraved by Hogarth and published in 1732. The original oil paintings were sold by Hogarth to Alderman Beckford in 1745, and are all generally supposed to have perished in the Fonthill fire of 1755, although the fire-damaged original of this scene reappeared at auction in 1991.

47 FRANS SNYDERS (1579–1657)
A Still-life with Fruit and a Cockatoo, Panel, Signed

Frans Snyders ran a large studio, and many of his paintings may have received only his partial attention. The Ascott *Still-life,* however, is of fine quality and the only known example of his work to include a cockatoo, a rare species in seventeenth-century Europe. Hella Robels dates the picture to the 1620s.

50

51

48 JAN ASSELIJN (AFTER 1610–52)

A Landscape with Peasants, Signed
The golden colour and suffused light of the landscape, as well as the small antique ruin in the centre background, identify this as a work of Asselijn's Italianate style. Asselijn probably went to Rome after 1635, but was north of the Alps by 1644, as he married in Lyon by the end of that year, and this would have been painted after that date.

49 SIR FRANCIS GRANT, PRA (1802–78)

Four Brothers of the de Rothschild Family Following Hounds
The four brothers depicted are the sons of Nathan Mayer de Rothschild, who had settled in England in 1798. In front is Nathaniel; following him and jumping a ditch is Lionel; behind are Mayer and Anthony. The de Rothschild staghounds are seen in full cry in the Vale of Aylesbury, with Creslow Great Ground, then the largest unenclosed field in the country, in the background.

FURNITURE AND WORKS OF ART

50 Louis XV ormolu-mounted parquetry bureau by Jean-Henri Riesener (1734–1806).

51 A boxwood thermometer and barometer carved with the initials 'L de R' (Leopold de Rothschild) and dated 1895.

52 A pair of Louis XVI-style ormolu-mounted tulipwood parquetry and marquetry side-cabinets with Spanish brocatelle marble tops, *c.*1880.

53 *On top of the side-cabinets* a pair of bronze groups, showing a lion attacking a bull and a lion attacking a stallion, after Giambologna, late seventeenth century to early eighteenth.

54 A pair of Louis XVI ormolu-mounted tulipwood *encoignures* (corner cupboards) with *brèche d'Alep* marble tops and acanthus foliage mounts, *c.*1775.

55 A late Louis XV ormolu-mounted tulipwood, sycamore and marquetry *secrétaire à abattant* (writing cabinet) stamped 'F Rubestuck JME' (1722–85) with a canted rectangular grey-veined marble top.

56 A pair of Louis XVI terracotta groups, probably late eighteenth century, each with a putto wrestling with a satyr, on a gilt wood and carved base.

55

57

57 *Below the stairs* is an Italian late eighteenth-century walnut cross-banded commode with tulipwood arabesque foliage in the manner of Maggiolini.

58 Part of a suite of George II walnut seat furniture, *c.*1740, with beaded acanthus and claw-and-ball feet, upholstered in contemporary needlework of coloured leaves on a brown ground.

59 A pair of silver-plated wall sconces.

60 A carved mahogany George II side-table (*c.*1740) with pierced acanthus apron to the centre on the front. The legs terminate in lion-claw feet.

CERAMICS

61 *At the far end of the lobby* is a rare green-and-amber glazed Chinese pottery basin of the Northern Song (960–1127) or Jin (1115–1234) dynasty.

56

THE COMMON ROOM

In the late 1880s James Williams, Devey's former partner, remodelled this as a drawing room with an elaborate plaster ceiling and inglenook fireplace, and a large timber-framed conservatory opening off it to the west. The conservatory disappeared in 1912, when Walter Godfrey added the drawing room (now Porcelain Room), and in the late 1930s Anthony and Yvonne de Rothschild radically simplified the decoration. The only trace of Devey's work surviving inside the house is the frieze, which bears mottoes such as 'Keep good company and be one of the number', 'He lacks most that longs most', 'It's an ill dog that deserves not a bone' and 'When the wine is in the wit is over'.

The fireplace was installed during Anthony and Yvonne's redecoration and dates from the Renaissance. The book alcove to its right was formerly a bay window. The room was redecorated by Robert Kime in 1997. At that date the four wooden door cases with entablatures were reinstated, based on old photographs.

PICTURES

62 CIRCLE OF DIRCK MAES (1659–1717)
Soldiers Attacking a Convoy, Panel
Although previously attributed to Jan Asselijn (after 1610–52), the extensive and finely detailed Italianate landscape points to an artist in the circle of Maes. The delicately drawn figures, as well as the types of the horses, also suggest Maes.

63 ATTRIBUTED TO AELBERT CUYP (1620–91)
A Peasant Boy with Cattle and Sheep, Panel, Inscribed: *A. cüyp*
The scene is the bank of the River Maas, with the tower of the Huis te Merwede in the distance. Similar subjects of herdsmen disrobing on the banks of a river attributed to Cuyp are known, but as yet the authenticity of this group of pictures has not been securely established. The

66

67

Ascott painting is in good condition and has generally been accepted as autograph.

64 ATTRIBUTED TO JAN BOECKHORST (1604–68)
Hélène Fourment, Panel

Previously attributed to Rubens, this lively portrait is of his second wife, Hélène Fourment, whom Rubens married in 1630. Other versions of the picture exist, some ascribed to Rubens, confirming its popularity.

Boeckhorst was an assistant of Rubens, known for the particular elegance with which he painted hands, as well as for the fluid quality of his brushwork, seen here in the highlights of the hair.

65 J. M. W. TURNER, RA (1775–1851)
Cicero at his Villa

According to William Chubb, Turner was inspired by Richard Wilson's version of the same subject and based the painting on drawings he made at Tivoli in 1828. Cecilia Powell has noted Roman sketches of 1819 that Turner also incorporated into this ancient Italian landscape. Although the setting is fairly faithfully reproduced, the grandeur of the Classical buildings and the theatrical pose of the melancholy philosopher bear witness to the greatness of Turner's invention. Turner referred to the fate of Cicero in a lecture thus: 'In acute anguish he retired, and as he lived he died neglected.' Exhibited at the Royal Academy in 1839.

66 FLORENTINE SCHOOL (*c*.1550–75)
A Youth, Panel

For long considered to be by Bronzino or Pontormo, this remarkable portrait is close to those of Francesco Salviati (1510–63), but it may be by a slightly later artist, such as Mirabello Cavalori (1535–after 1578). The background has been over painted, but the figure seems to be well preserved, and the artist has captured the sitter in the act of pulling on a glove while fixing us with his direct gaze.

67 LUDOLPH DE JONGH (1616–79)
A Lady Receiving a Letter, Signed

De Jongh's subject is probably the unhappy fate of the presumptuous suitor. The young lady is coolly gazing at the suitor's messenger, while her maids are engaged in domestic duties, and in the foreground an amorous dog is repulsed by a bitch. The action is paralleled in the painting hanging in the background, of *Diana and Actaeon* (based on an engraving by Antonio Tempesta): Actaeon was devoured by his own hounds after accidentally coming upon Diana bathing with her nymphs. De Jongh's work is little studied and difficult to date. This picture may have been painted around 1658, when he produced his finest compositions, under the influence of his junior, Pieter de Hooch (1629–84).

68

72

68 JAN VAN DER HEYDEN (1637–1712)

A Square in an Imaginary Flemish Town, Panel, Signed
Despite van der Heyden's meticulous rendering of detail
in this cityscape, this is in fact an assembled caprice. The
tower in the left background is recognisable as Nijen-
rode Castle, while the Baroque façade in the right background is that of the so-called 'House of Isabella' in
Brussels. The church and shop in the foreground are
familiar from a similar composition now in Los Angeles,
dated 1676. The well-drawn but robust figures are probably also by the artist. The two Dominican friars would
never have been seen in a Dutch town, which the picture
was previously said to represent.

69 NICOLAES MAES (1634–93)

The Milk Girl, Signed
Maes was fond of dark ruddy colours, in which bright
light is reflected or to which it adheres. The metal milk
jug mirrors the curve of the milkmaid's ankle, while the
milk sold to the housewife absorbs the light and shines
white. The intimacy of the early morning scene is
heightened by the transaction taking place in a quiet

corner, to which the other street-sellers in the background
are oblivious. Maes was indebted to Rembrandt for his
powerful effects of light and shadow, but the peculiar
insistence on domesticity is the artist's own contribution.

70 MEINDERT HOBBEMA (1638–1709)

Cottages in a Wood, Panel, Signed
Hobbema's best work satisfies the Dutch city-dweller's
keen demand for an idealised vision of nature. Hobbema
is still reliant here on his teacher Jacob van Ruisdael for
imagery but approaches the grander scale and lighter
tonality that mark his late works. Painted *c.*1662–4, this
is a prelude to re-elaborations of the theme such as *The
Village among Trees,* signed and dated 1665, now in the
Frick Collection in New York.

71 FORMERLY ATTRIBUTED TO LORENZO LOTTO (*c.*1480–1556)

Portrait of a Young Man
For a picture of this style and period not to be painted
on panel is highly unusual, and there is no indication
of its having been transferred from panel to canvas.

Although Bernard Berenson attributes the portrait to Lorenzo Lotto, and it was exhibited as such at the Lotto exhibition in Venice in 1953, this is no longer generally accepted.

72 STUDIO OF SIR PETER PAUL RUBENS (1577–1640)
The Madonna and Child, Panel transferred to canvas
The picture, which has areas of damage and retouching, is no longer accepted as an autograph work. Prof. Julius Held suggested that it may come from the Rubens workshop.

SCULPTURE

73 HOLME CARDWELL (B.1815, ACTIVE 1836–56)
Greyhounds Playing, c.1844, Bronze
A writer to the *Gentleman's Magazine* in 1844 recorded that, on a visit to Cardwell's studio, he had found the sculptor executing the original of this group, and that it 'showed a keen observation of nature and great powers'. It was the kind of subject with which his fellow-Northener, Joseph Gott (1786–1860), had made his name, and Cardwell may have been seeking to emulate him.

74 AUGUSTE RODIN (1840–1917)
The Age of Bronze,1876, Bronze, cast by Alexis Rudier
The original, life-size version of this (now in the Ny Carlsberg Glyptotek, Copenhagen) was created in Brussels between 1875 and 1877, but sent for exhibition in Paris. It was Rodin's first masterpiece, but also brought him his first notoriety. The main reason was that he was falsely accused of having made it with the aid of a life-cast. Another was that the figure – originally conceived as a vanquished warrior – was given neither attributes nor title; the present title was arrived at only after several others had been foisted on it.

75

Alexis Rudier was Rodin's favoured bronze-founder, whose foundry continued to cast his works after his death.

FURNITURE AND WORKS OF ART

75 *Either side of the French window* is a pair of Louis XVI harewood cabinets (*c.*1775) with latticework parquetry and white marble tops surrounded by an ormolu gallery. One is a secretaire; the other contains shelves. The latter cabinet is stamped 'A. Weisweiler' (1740–1820).

76 Part of a set of George II figured walnut side-chairs attributed to William Hallett, *c.*1740, each with a cartouche-shaped back, needlework-covered seat and claw-and-ball feet.

77 A Louis XV inlaid desk of shaped outline with ormolu mounts. The four drawers and the sides are inlaid with marquetry panels of sprays of tulips and other flowers. Attributed to the *ébéniste du roi* Jean-François Oeben (1721–63).

82

77

78 A French ormolu- and porcelain-mounted tricoteuse (work-table) with tray top with bowed ends and parquetry ground, first half of nineteenth century.

79 *To the left of the far door* is a royal late Louis XV ormolu-mounted tulipwood, sycamore and marquetry commode. Stamped 'M. G. Cramer' (active 1771–94), it was made for the Comtesse de Provence's use at Fontainebleau in 1771.

80 *Standing on it* are two giallo marble groups of *Lionesses Playing* and a *Lioness with Cub* on oval plinths, seventeenth century.

81 A pair of Queen Anne-style gilt-gesso pier-glasses with shell decoration on their crests.

82 A Louis XV ormolu-mounted kingwood commode by Claude-Charles Saunier (1735–1807) with trellis parquetry and brown-and-white marble top.

83 *Either side of the fireplace* are two Louis XV parquetry library tables, *c*.1765. They have a writing slide at each end. The frieze is inlaid with key-pattern marquetry. One of them is stamped 'JME' by the *ébéniste* Philippe-Claude Montigny (1734–1800).

84 An early George III mahogany reading-table of square form with hinged top and tripod base, *c*.1760.

85 A mahogany reading-stand with rectangular adjustable top, mid-eighteenth century.

86 A George III mahogany music stand, *c*.1770.

CERAMICS

87 *To the left of the doorway* is a pair of iron-red painted Chinese porcelain vases of the Kangxi period (1662–1722), converted into pot-pourri jars with Louis XVI ormolu mounts.

88 *On the mantelpiece* are three other pot-pourri vessels of Chinese porcelain with French ormolu mounts. The larger vessel is composed of two Chinese bowls with crackled glazes, the smaller ones of flowerpots and stands, all dating from the early eighteenth century and mounted shortly after. These three pieces do not form part of the collection of Chinese ceramics assembled by Anthony de Rothschild but were inherited. Similar examples can be seen in Waddesdon Manor.

THE PORCELAIN ROOM

Walter Godfrey created this room in 1912 as the drawing room, on the site of the former conservatory at the western end of the house. He installed light oak panelling and a Jacobean-style fireplace, which was replaced by the present, simpler marble version during Anthony de Rothschild's remodelling in the late 1930s. The room was converted for the display of the important Ascott collection of Chinese ceramics in 1997 under the direction of Robert Kime, who designed the chinoiserie bamboo cabinets.

PICTURES

89 ANDREA DEL SARTO (1486–1531)
The Madonna and Child with St John, Panel
Traditionally known as the *Madonna del Fries,* after Count Joseph von Fries, who bought the picture in Italy. It was subsequently acquired by Charles, 3rd Marquess of Londonderry, after his return from the embassy in Vienna, to which city Joseph's brother had taken it. It was accepted by Crowe and Cavalcaselle, Berenson,

Waterhouse and Garlick but was regarded by Freedberg as 'an excellent copy' of a lost original of *c.*1520. Shearman catalogues it as the original of the composition and dates it *c.*1521, in style close to the Vienna *Pietà* and the lost *Madonna di Porta Pinti.* The authoritative verdict of Shearman has since been confirmed by the cleaning of the picture by John Brealey in 1969 and by subsequent publications. Goethe saw the painting in the Fries collection in 1787 and considered it 'an incredibly beautiful picture; without having seen it, one could not conceive of such a thing', while Waterhouse called it 'one of the least-known major Italian works in England'.

FURNITURE

90 *By the windows* is a suite of George III mahogany furniture comprising a settee and four chairs upholstered in tapestry with flowers and landscapes on a blue ground. (Two other chairs from this suite are in the Lobby.)

91 *Left of the bay window* is a late Louis XV *bonheur-du-jour* (lady's writing-table) inlaid with utensils and flowering

94

vases, and with an ormolu Greek frieze to the drawer

92 *Right of the bay window* is an ormolu-mounted Louis XV writing-table with four drawers all inlaid with utensils, *c*.1765.

93 *In front of the west window* is a particularly important Louis XV black lacquer fall-front secretaire of shaped outline with red marble top, decorated with villages against mountains, and finely chased ormolu mounts. Stamped 'BVRB, JME' for Bernard van Risenburgh

(1700–65) and '+Joseph+' for Joseph Baumhauer (d. 1772), who may have repaired the piece.

Around the room are fine late seventeenth-century (Kangxi) Chinese coromandel lacquer panels.

CERAMICS

To the left of the doorway the first case shows porcelains of the *famille verte* and *famille jaune* dating from the Kangxi period (1662–1722). The pear-shaped vase on the central shelf is flanked by two particularly exquisite vases on marbled tripod pedestals, whose fine porcelain body is very skilfully painted with birds perched on flowering branches. This shape, with fixed stands, is particularly rare. The two lanterns on either side, which are lavishly painted with figure scenes, represent a technical *tour de force*. They are made of eggshell-thin, and therefore highly translucent, porcelain.

The second case contains a group of Ming dynasty *fahua* wares, dating mainly from the sixteenth century. (**94**) The best example of this ware in the house, and one of the finest in existence, is on the bottom left-hand shelf. Its elaborate decoration is outlined in trails of slip, with parts in applied slip relief, all with incised detail and picked out in an elegant colour scheme of a pale (and virtually unique) copper-red, turquoise, green and purple on a dark blue ground. The complex Daoist figure scene shows the three Star Gods of Longevity, Affluence and Happiness playing a board game, with the Queen Mother of the West approaching from the left with four attendants, and the Eight Immortals approaching from the right.

The ceramic sculptures in this case include two figures of Shou Lao, the Daoist God of Longevity, with outsized forehead, seated on a deer, which symbolises good

fortune, and accompanied by a crane, another symbol of longevity. On the shelf below is a figure of the Bodhisattva Avalokitesvara, revered in China as Guanyin, Goddess of Mercy, seated on a pedestal, crowned and bejewelled, identified by a tiny figure of the Buddha in her tiara, and with an elaborate mandorla. A Daoist immortal holding a lotus flower is at the top left, and two rare figures of Buddha's main disciples are at the top right: Kasyapa, shown as an older man, and Ananda, as younger. Both wear monk's robes and have their hands raised in prayer.

The fireplace houses a massive fish bowl painted in *wucai* ('five colours') with mandarin ducks in a lotus pond

– symbol of marital bliss – and inscribed below the rim with the Wanli reign mark (1573–1619).

The third case shows in the centre a tilework figure intended to be placed as guardian on the roof, and two Ming dynasty vases. The central vase is one of the largest existing *fahua* vases, with elaborate applied peony handles. The piece below it is a rare temple vase with a documentary inscription stating that it was commissioned by an official from a village near Xi'an, in Shaanxi province. The piece was cut down and later re-assembled with champlevé enamel handles. The shelves on either side contain porcelain figures of the eighteenth century. On the top and bottom shelves are seated figures of popular deities dressed in officials' robes, some of them with real hair inserted as beards and moustaches; in the third row are standing figures of the Star Gods of Affluence and Longevity: Lu Xing with hair tied in two buns, and Shou Xing with tall forehead. The next shelves below show the Daoist and the Buddhist mother goddess: Xi Wang Mu, the Queen Mother of the West, on the left, unusually depicted with a green-glazed face, and (**95**) Guanyin with a child on the right.

On display in *the fourth case* are *fahua* wares of the Ming dynasty together with monochrome turquoise-glazed wares of the Qing (1644–1911). (**96**) At the top are two unusually large (and very heavy) sixteenth-century figures of the Daoist immortals Lan Caihe, with a flower basket, and Zhongli Quan, with wide-open gown. These would originally have belonged to a set of eight, but no other matching figures are recorded. The turquoise-ground vase on the central shelf, in the form of a bottle

97

98

gourd and decorated with lotus scrolls, is one of the earliest pieces of this type, dating from the beginning of the sixteenth century. (**97**) The peach-shaped wine ewers on the central shelves further down, which have no opening except for the thin spout, were filled through a hole in the bottom that leads into a tall tube inside the vessel, so that no liquid spills out when they are turned upright. Such ewers are known in the West as 'Cadogan teapots', after English pottery copies made at the Rockingham factory. The Chinese versions would, however, have been used for strong wine, which was drunk hot. (**98**) Near by are two decorative pyramids of auspicious fruit: peaches as symbols of long life, and pomegranates representing the blessing of many children. The large barrel-shaped items on the bottom shelves, decorated in turquoise and purple with peacocks and peonies, were used as garden seats.

Displayed in the bay is the famous blue-glazed storage jar and cover of the Tang dynasty (618–907). The cobalt pigment used for the glaze, which had to be imported from the Middle East, was so precious that it was used mainly for smaller vessels or in combination with other colours. The application of the several glaze layers on this piece, suggestive of a hilly landscape, is particularly attractive.

The fifth case includes more *fahua* wares of the Ming and some figures of the Qing dynasty. The second shelf from the top on the right-hand side contains a piece of a different type altogether, although similar in appearance. This ovoid vase, which is painted with panels of cranes in brown, ochre and turquoise on a white ground, is a late example of the more rustic 'Cizhou' stonewares, which

were made for daily use in north China since the tenth century. The present piece dates from the fifteenth or sixteenth century. The pairs of figures of Guanyin, the Buddhist Goddess of Mercy, seated on a lotus pedestal, and of Shou Lao, the Daoist God of Longevity, with characteristic elongated forehead, were made somewhat later, in the early Qing dynasty (late seventeenth century or early eighteenth) and are finer in material than most other pieces in this vitrine; one hand of one figure was replaced in silver.

The last case in this room contains vessels of both Ming and Qing dynasties. Most remarkable are the beaker-shaped vase at the top centre and the two bowls in the centre left and right. Of the same type as porcelains of the *famille jaune* and *famille noire,* with their yellow or black ground colours, the designs on these vessels are reserved on an exceptional pale aubergine ground. The turquoise bowl at the bottom centre is a rare piece from the Imperial kilns, and is inscribed on the base with the Jiajing reign mark (1522–66).

THE SMALL LOBBY

This small room connects the Common Room with the Library, which lies to its north.

FURNITURE

99 A late Louis XV ormolu-mounted parquetry and marquetry commode with a breche violet marble top, *c.*1775.

TEXTILES

100 A needlework panel with a design of vases on a wrought-iron trellis.

THE LIBRARY

This originally formed the billiard room, which was added to the north of the present Common Room by James Williams in the late 1880s. In the late 1930s Anthony and Yvonne de Rothschild turned it into an oak-panelled library. The inset bookcases contain a collection of artists' books assembled by them in the 1930s. The woodwork was lightened under the direction of Robert Kime in 1997.

The dummy book spines on the door leading to the Library Passage include: *Truth is Stranger than Fiction,* by Baron Münchausen (the notorious teller of tall tales); *Young Husband on Passive Obedience*; *Log Book of the Ark*; *What I Saw in the Dark,* by A. Bat; *A Smooth Passage,* by A. Swell; and *D. Cline on Consumption*.

PICTURES

101   MANNER OF CORNEILLE DE LA HAYE, CALLED CORNEILLE DE LYON (ACTIVE 1533–75)
Portrait of a Lady, perhaps Queen Eleanor of France (1498–1558), Panel, Dated 1550
The elaborate costume and jewels indicate a person of some distinction. Although Corneille also painted the rich bourgeoisie and the nobility, few individuals other than royalty could afford such extravagance. In 1534 he was made *painctre de la Royne Helienor* (Queen Eleanor, the second wife of François I), and in 1541 he became *peintre du Dauphin* (later Henri II). Curiously, however, although there are a number of portraits by Corneille of ladies of Queen Eleanor's court, not even a copy of a portrait by him of the queen herself is otherwise known. Another version of this portrait was on the art market in 1989, as a portrait of Jacqueline de Monsel.

102   ATTRIBUTED TO FRANS POURBUS THE YOUNGER (1569–1622)
A Woman in a White Bonnet, Panel
Heavy restoration and repainting make an attribution difficult, but this is close in style to other portraits by Frans Pourbus.

103   ATTRIBUTED TO LUDGER TOM RING THE YOUNGER (1522–84)
A Small Child, Panel, Dated 1583
This is extremely close to a portrait, possibly of the same child and wearing an identical dress, in a private collec-

111

112

tion in Stuttgart. The Stuttgart picture is ascribed with reservation to Ludger Tom Ring the Elder by Riewerts and Pieper. The date precludes the possibility of the Ascott picture being by the elder Ring, but there is much in favour of an attribution to the Ring the Younger, who died a year after it was painted. Analogies to the stiffly posed figure with its round cheeks can easily be found in his portraits. The composition differs from the Stuttgart portrait in not showing the sitter's hands, but it has evidently been cut at the bottom.

104 JOHN WOOTTON (1682–1764)

Racing on Newmarket Heath

Wootton, the leading horse-painter in England in the first half of the eighteenth century, made several paintings of Newmarket races, and there was a sketch of *A View of Newmarket Course* on the first day of his studio sale in 1761. Most often, however, he showed horses being exercised, from a high vantage point on Warren Hill. The present picture is an unusual and pioneering view of an actual race lower down on the heath.

105 JAN WIJNANTS (1631/2–84)

Figures on a Road by a Wood, Signed and dated 1668

Wijnants's landscapes are distinctively arranged: the trees are centred, and the landscape recedes behind them on either side; he repeatedly used the motif of a gnarled tree with a dead tree trunk at its base for dramatic effect. Both Smith and de Groot attribute the figures to Johannes Lingelbach, who collaborated regularly with Wijnants. Despite the appealing quality of his gentle landscapes, Wijnants was not commercially successful and died in debt.

106 CORNELIS DECKER (BEFORE 1625–78)

A Woodland Scene, Initialled and dated 1667

Decker was one of a large group of followers of the landscapist Jacob van Ruisdael and was influenced by his poetic rendering of natural forces. The figures have been attributed to Adriaen van Ostade, who occasionally collaborated with Decker.

107 GEORGE MORLAND (1762/3–1804)

'Rural Life'

Morland is now better known for his bohemian lifestyle

113

114

than for his pictures, whose 'total absence of any intellectual qualities have made them always very popular' (Ellis Waterhouse). In the best of them, however, of which this is one, he combines an easy – but, in fact, artful – naturalism with a fresh handling of paint and colour that only Gainsborough among his contemporaries could surpass.

108 FRANS VAN MIERIS THE ELDER (1635–81)
Portrait of a Man, Panel, Monogrammed
Van Mieris's small panel is carefully composed to accentuate its arched-top format, with an arched door frame in the background and the sitter himself in a pose that imitates a semicircle. Nauman suggests that the portrait is the companion to a similarly arched-top *Portrait of a Woman* (signed *Fr. van Mieris* and dated 1673) that is now lost. He discounts the view of earlier writers that the sitter is the Flemish artist Frans Wouters. The letter the sitter holds remains tantalisingly illegible, but the map, inkpot and pen, and glimpse of a library through the arch, all suggest a gentleman–scholar.

A late work, this portrait shows off van Mieris's consummate talent for rendering silk fabrics.

109 CASPAR NETSCHER (*c.*1635/6–84)
A Lady as a Shepherdess, Panel
An exact replica, of similar measurements but with a different face, signed and dated 'C. Netscher Fec. 1681', was in the Lilienfeld Collection in Vienna in 1917. The fine quality of the Ascott picture indicates an autograph variant, as the painter is known to have offered pre-painted standard poses for his sitters.

110 FRANS VAN MIERIS THE ELDER (1635–81)
Portrait of a Young Man, Copper
Nauman rejects the former identification of the sitter as Greffier Fagel (in the later sale of whose collection in London in 1801 it is first recorded) and dates the picture to the 1670s. The picture is a fine example of *fijnschilderij*, the refined painting technique whereby no brushwork is visible. Van Mieris makes use of the Flemish convention of the speaking or gesturing portrait; his sitter seems to be caught in movement, further enhancing the lifelike quality of the image.

111 GIOVANNI BATTISTA TIEPOLO (1696–1770)
The Assumption of the Virgin, Painted roundel
The composition is close to a modello (preserved in the cathedral at San Daniele del Friuli, just north of Udine)

115

116

for a ceiling fresco by Tiepolo in the Church of the Fratta at Friuli, which was never executed. Morassi associates this study with three other modelli for the ceiling, on the basis of iconography (the Assumption) and style (dating them all to 1735). It may have belonged to the artist's widow, Cecilia Guardi, an inveterate gambler, who is said to have lost her entire collection of Tiepolo sketches on one throw of the dice. It was later owned by Edward Cheney (1803–84), of Badger Hall, Shropshire, who assembled no fewer than 19 such sketches.

112 THOMAS GAINSBOROUGH, RA (1727–88)

Supposed Portrait of Lady Mary Bruce, Duchess of Richmond (1740–96)
John Hayes has called this 'one of the most ravishing of Gainsborough's late romantic portraits. ... The enigmatic smile and slightly distant expression heighten the poetic mood of the canvas.' The supposed sitter was the daughter and co-heir of Charles, 4th Earl of Elgin and 3rd Earl of Aylesbury, by his third marriage, in 1739, to Caroline, daughter of the 4th Duke of Argyll. She married in 1757 Charles, 3rd Duke of Richmond and Lennox. There were no children of the marriage, and the title devolved upon a nephew.

The picture has been called a 'late London work' by Waterhouse, and ascribed more precisely by Hayes to 1786–7, when Lady Mary would have been over 45 years old. In an endeavour to resolve the discrepancy between the sitter's apparent age and the evident date of the picture, it has been suggested that she is the wife, Lady Louisa Gordon Lennox, daughter of the 2nd Duke of Richmond, and not the sister-in-law of Thomas Conolly, to whom this picture is said to have belonged. But neither the dark-haired Hugh Douglas Hamilton pastel of her at Springhill, Co. Londonderry, nor the Romney portrait of her at Goodwood, Sussex, bears this out. However, nor can one detect any resemblance to the equally dark-haired sitter in the Chardinesque Reynolds of *Mary, Duchess of Richmond, Sewing,* which is likewise at Goodwood.

When the portrait was purchased by Anthony de Rothschild, the sitter was shown wearing a bonnet. Through the use of ultra-violet light, it was found that the headpiece had been added later by another artist, probably in order to conceal the sitter's ill-regarded red hair. Anthony had the bonnet removed to uncover the original Gainsborough that is seen today.

117

118

SCULPTURE

**113 JOSEPH ROSSET (1706–86) OR ONE OF HIS SONS,
JACQUES, CLAUDE AND FRANÇOIS FOSSET**

Voltaire (c. 1694–1778), Marble statuette on a Siena marble
pedestal

When this statuette was auctioned in the immense
Hamilton Place sale of 1882, it was thought to be by
Houdon, who produced the classic life-size images of the
writer. It is much more likely to be a work of either Joseph
Rosset, known as Rosset Du Pont, whom Voltaire
consented to sit for, and also helped by taking off his wig
whilst doing so when playing chess, or one of his three
sculptor-sons: Jacques-Joseph (1742–1809), Claude-
Antoine (1749–1818) or François-Marie (1752–1824) in the
Franche-Comté. Joseph Rosset specialised in making
busts of the Encylopédistes (Voltaire, d'Alembert,
Rousseau and Montesquieu), and Frederick the Great
declared: 'There is nobody who can imbue a bust with life
like the sculptor from Franche-Comté.' But it may have
been Claude-Antoine who extended the likeness of
Voltaire to his whole figure.

114 An Egyptian basalt head on a marble stand, 26th
Dynasty.

115 AUGUSTE RODIN (1840–1917)

The Thinker, 1880, Bronze

This is a reduction of Rodin's most celebrated sculpture,
which was originally conceived as the focal point of what
became his life's work: the sculpted bronze portals for the
Musée des Arts Décoratifs in Paris, commissioned in 1880,
but never installed, with Dante's Inferno as their theme,
and consequently known as *The Gates of Hell*. At first
intended to represent Dante himself, he became the
generalised figure of a poet – and then of Man – pondering
the great questions of life and death. Appropriately therefore, a cast was placed over Rodin's own grave.

116 AUGUSTE RODIN (1840–1917)

Eve, c.1881/1899, Bronze

All Rodin's earliest serious sculpture was based on the
male figure or head. Only in 1879 did he make a group and
a bust using his mistress, Rose Beuret, as a model. The next
year he began a life-size *Eve*, as a pendant to *Adam*, for *The
Gates of Hell*. His model, a certain Madame Albruzzezzi,
became pregnant, and Rodin had to suspend his modelling; that Eve did not finally appear until the Salon of 1899.
Meanwhile, however, he had made his 30-inch version,
which proved to be immensely popular.

126

127

117 A gilt-bronze figure of Guanyin, Goddess of Mercy, Tang dynasty (AD 618–907).

118 A bronze of a Bodhisattva, Sukhothai, sixteenth century.

FURNITURE

119 *Around the room* are four early nineteenth-century chairs, with painted vignettes of racing scenes on their top rails, made by J. N. Sartorius in 1809 (a further pair are in the Library Passage).

120 *In the centre of the room* is an early nineteenth-century mahogany pedestal desk, possibly Scottish, with red leather top, gadrooned edge, six frieze drawers and twelve pedestal drawers.

121 Two mahogany George II-style oval pie-crust tilt-top tables.

122 *In the bay* a figured walnut concertina-action card table, nineteenth century.

123 A George III mahogany serving-table with six square tapering fluted legs, attributed to Thomas Chippendale, *c.*1775.

TEXTILES

124–5 The carpets include a seventeenth-century Isfahan with its maroon ground centre decorated with blue, yellow and green flowers, and a sixteenth-century Isfahan carpet having a pink ground centre with floral design in blue and yellow.

CERAMICS

126 The bright purple-glazed Jun ware flowerpot *on the desk* is outstanding for its vivid glaze colour. It dates from the fourteenth or fifteenth century, when such vivid glaze colours were still rare, and is inscribed on the base with the numeral 1, indicating the largest of ten sizes.

127 The pair of polychrome painted *wucai* ('five-colour') vases *on side-tables*, pear-shaped and with 'garlic-head' mouths, and decorated with lotus-pond scenes, are Imperial porcelains of the Wanli period (1573–1619) and are inscribed on the rim with the reign mark. *Wucai* porcelains, which required several firings for different colours, were the most prestigious ceramics of this period.

128 *On the window-ledge* above Rodin's *Thinker* are three pairs of vases of the *famille verte*. The tall pair of 'rouleau' vases is particularly impressive, not only for its remarkable size but particularly for its superbly painted large-scale lotus-pond design.

129 The impressive yellow-and-green temple figure, probably representing the God of Literature, dates from the late Ming dynasty (sixteenth or early seventeenth century). A successful firing of a figure of this size and complexity was a remarkable feat on the part of the potters.

THE LIBRARY PASSAGE
This passage brings you back to the Lobby.

PICTURES
130 FRANÇOIS BOUCHER (1703–70)
The Arts: Sculpture, Signed and dated 1758
One of a series of four pictures of the Arts, represented by
putti with the attributes of their art. The others, which
are neither signed nor dated, are *Music*, *Painting* and
Poetry. Here, the bust of the child is painted from a sculpture by Jacques Saly, of which there are numerous versions in marble, bronze and terracotta, of both eight-
eenth- and nineteenth-century origin. Her identity – if
she was ever intended to have one at all, as opposed to
being simply a genre study – remains uncertain, as does
the reason for Boucher's predilection for incorporating
depictions of the bust in his paintings. All four pictures
were in the first posthumous sale, in Paris in 1870, of the
collection of Prince Anatole Demidoff, husband of Prin-
cess Mathilde Bonaparte, from his Villa San Donato,
outside Florence.

130

136

131 MANNER OF NICOLAS DE LARGILLIERRE (1656–1746)

Portrait of a Man, Copper

Previously catalogued as a portrait of the Regent, Philippe, Duc d'Orléans (1674–1723). On the basis of costume, the sitter must indeed be French, but the full ribbon bow he wears indicates a date in the late 1680s. The style is close to the work of Largillierre, a French painter trained in Antwerp and England, who eventually settled in Paris and rivalled Rigaud for commissions from the nobility and financiers.

132 AFTER PIETRO VANNUCCI, CALLED IL PERUGINO (1445/50–1523)

The Head of Saint Apollonia, Panel

The head of Saint Apollonia derives from Perugino's *Virgin and Child with Saints Michael the Archangel, Catherine of Alexandria, Apollonia and John the Baptist* in the Pinacoteca Nazionale, Bologna. The altarpiece, which is signed, came originally from the Cappella Scarani in San Giovanni in Monte and was painted *c.*1497.

133 A George III mahogany centre table, *c.*1760, with rectangular top, and now fitted with a bronze showcase.

134 A Louis XV *régulateur* (clock), signed 'Chevallier aux Thuilleries' in a shaped kingwood and parquetry case, *c.*1735. Surmounted by an ormolu figure of Cupid and with other ornate features on the case.

135 A Louis XV shaped *cartonnier* (desk), *c.*1730, with leather-covered drawers standing on a tulipwood cabinet with cupboards at either end with gilt-bronze mounts. This is surmounted by an ormolu figure of Diana and a hound, with to one side a boar and hound and to the other a stag and hound. It also incorporates a clock signed 'Champion à Paris'.

136 Two *Cambodian heads,* tenth and eleventh century, one bronze and one limestone.

137

CERAMICS

In the vitrine at the head of the passage are the earliest examples of Chinese ceramics at Ascott – burial pottery from the Han (206 BC–AD 220) and Tang (618–907) dynasties. All these objects were made not for use but for burial in tombs, the vessels filled with provisions and the figures and models as substitutes for the real thing.

On the top shelf can be seen a Han dynasty horse's head, whose separately made body and legs are missing, and a Tang dynasty tripod incense-burner, basins and a storage jar.

(**137**) The central shelf shows only Tang dynasty vessels and figures of hunting hounds. The blue glaze derived from cobalt was the most precious pigment at the time, since it had to be imported from Persia, while the pigments for the more common *sancai* ('three-colour') palette in tones of green, yellow and brown were all available locally.

On the bottom shelf are a model of a draw well, a triple bowl and an incense-burner with pierced cover imitating the bronze examples in use at the time which, when emitting smoke, would symbolise a paradise mountainous island enveloped in clouds. These three pieces, which date from the Han dynasty, were all covered with a similar green glaze, which in two cases, however, acquired an attractive iridescent silvery patina as a result of burial. The fierce-looking mythical guardian animal dates from the sixth or seventh century, and the two figures of boars from the Tang dynasty.

The large vases and jars *on top of the vitrines*, painted in the colour schemes of the *famille verte* (on a white ground), *famille noire* (black ground) and *famille jaune* (yellow ground), date from the Kangxi reign (1662–1722) of the last Chinese dynasty, the Qing. They were popular particularly among Western collectors of the early twentieth century, and those of the *famille noire*, of which the large jar and cover with its luxuriant garden scene with decorative rockwork is a particularly fine example, were the most highly valued Chinese porcelains in the West.

Most of the vessels *in the vitrine on the outer wall* can be dated between the tenth and fourteenth centuries, although the elephants (bottom left) and the white vase (bottom right) are much later.

On the left are two unusual bright green glazed vessels of the Liao dynasty (907–1125), a dynasty established by the Qidan, a non-Chinese people in the north-eastern part of China. One, with amber-coloured panels on either side, has a flattened body and horizontal straps for carrying it on a string; the other is in the shape of a leather bottle with a twisted-rope handle, its seams imitated by raised ribs. Both vessels reflect the nomadic origin of their makers. The pear-shaped green-glazed vase next to the latter dates from the Mongol Yuan dynasty (1279–1368) and is made in imitation of a contemporary bronze vessel.

(**138**) The most important group of vessels in this vitrine are the Jun wares of the Northern Song (960–1127) and Jin (1115–1234) dynasties, which are displayed towards the centre. This ceramic ware of north China, with its striking colouration in bright blue, often with deep purple splashes, simple shapes and absence of decoration, is particularly well represented at Ascott. On the right-hand side is also a pair of ivory-white bowls of the Song dynasty from the Ding kilns in Hebei province.

While these bowls were made in the north of China,

138

139

the lobed vase and the other pair of white bowls on the bottom shelf are roughly contemporary wares from Jingdezhen in the south, which are known as *gingbai* ('bluish-white') on account of the characteristic blue tinge of their glaze. Also made in southern China, by the Longquan kilns, are the grey-green 'celadon' bottle, top left, and a pair of similarly glazed bowls at the bottom, which date from the fifteenth and fourteenth centuries respectively.

The table case contains a particularly fine group of Jun vessels with bright lavender grey and purple glazes. It would appear that Anthony de Rothschild was particularly fond of this colour scheme, which is a leitmotif of his whole ceramic collection. The three circular and two rectangular basins would have been used in China as narcissus bowls or flowerpot stands and belong to a group of such mould-made flower vessels marked on the base with figures from 1 to 10, denoting their size. Their exact dating is still debated, but they are generally assumed to postdate the simpler wheel-shaped Jun wares of the Song dynasty, such as the tripod incense-burner, small dish and small jar with two handles also displayed in this case.

The rich assembly of vessels and figures *in the two vitrines on the inner wall* dates mainly from the Kangxi period of the Qing dynasty.

The small vitrine on the right shows vessels of the *famille verte*, including, on the bottom shelf, a particularly early jar with overall green waves, dating from the third quarter of the seventeenth century, and another jar of similar date, which, however, was later over-decorated in Europe in *famille noire* style, owing to the great popularity of such wares.

In the larger vitrine on the left are displayed, on the top shelf, a pair of Buddhist lions, peach-shaped wine ewers, which were filled through a tubular opening in the bottom, and various figures of Daoist immortals, originally made for Chinese house altars but which became a highly popular export commodity in the eighteenth century.

The central shelf holds two water droppers in the shape of dragon heads emerging from waves and various equestrian figures, including a particularly finely modelled one with yellow armour and real hair (a helmet perhaps lost). Most unusual are two figures of Luohan, which were rarely modelled in porcelain, each casually seated on a plinth with one leg raised; one is sleeping, the other smiling. They represent disciples of Buddha who have lived through all stages of rebirth and have reached nirvana, but who are not aspiring to Buddha-hood and are therefore remaining on earth. They are usually depicted in an unconventional, informal manner. A more conventional immortal is the Daoist Lü Dongbin, shown here with exquisitely modelled features, clad in a yellow robe and seated on a leaf.

The bottom shelf shows unusual wine ewers – one in the shape of a monkey sucking a peach, (**139**) and another pair in the form of stags – and an incense-burner in the form of a Buddhist lion, its green body shaped as a receptacle, its yellow head as a cover, its eyes and mouth pierced to emit smoke and its eyeballs loosely inserted and freely movable. The green-and-yellow *meiping* ('prunus-blossom bottle') in the centre belongs to a different era – the sixteenth century of the Ming dynasty – and with this colour scheme is a rare variant of the generally turquoise-and-purple *fahua*-type wares displayed through the house.

The mainly turquoise-glazed miniature vessels and figures *in the Queen Anne cabinet* range in date from the sixteenth century to the nineteenth. They include many water droppers that would have been used on a Chinese scholar's table for preparing his ink, which came in the form of a hard stick and had to be ground and mixed with water.

Chapter 6
The Garden

HISTORY

The garden at Ascott has always been among the property's best-known and most original features. Covering over 30 acres, it is an unusual blend of the formal and the natural. In many gardens the area nearest the house has the strongest architectural character, the regions further away being left more to nature, but at Ascott the reverse is true. The principal formal features – sundial, Madeira Walk, Venus Garden and Dutch Garden – are disposed in a chain along the south side of the grounds, while the area in front of the house is simply a smooth grass sward dotted with trees in a park-like manner. This arrangement reflects the original intention whereby the house, despite its size, aimed to keep some of the character of the old farmstead. The former orchard to the west of the house was carefully retained, and in front of the house topiary specimens were arranged, as they were thought to be consonant with the 'Old English' architecture of the place. The grander gardening gestures with sculptural fountains and elaborately planted flower beds were kept at arm's length and are not immediately visible from the house itself. This enhances their impact when they are encountered unexpectedly on a walk around the garden. Horticultural writers in the 1890s saw the Ascott garden as a striking combination of the 'ancient and modern' styles of gardening.

The other unusual aspect of the Ascott grounds is their array of brilliantly hued foliage, with a wide range of variegated and golden-leaved shrubs. This was probably a reflection of the Victorian and Edwardian Ascott season, which ran from November to May: coloured 'evergreens' were the most effective plants to have in the gardens in winter. There are Golden Privet, Golden

above
The north front of Ascott House

right
The Dutch Garden

Holly, Golden Cedar, Golden Box and Golden Cypress. Exuberant planting of coloured foliage also governed the choice of deciduous trees and shrubs, which included Golden Elm, Blue Larch, Copper Beech, Japanese Maple, Purple Berberis, Silver Willow and translucent Bronze-leaved Cotinus, creating an almost psychedelic collection of trees. These specimens are said to have been supplied originally by Veitch's of Chelsea, the celebrated Victorian nurseryman.

Leopold de Rothschild was himself a keen and talented gardener, and he was the moving force in the design and evolution of the garden, assisted by his head gardener, John Jennings, who was appointed in 1877 and worked at Ascott for over 30 years. George Devey's office seems only to have provided designs for the various structures. Walter Godfrey, who himself designed a formal area (since modified) at the west end of the house, stated categorically that Devey did not lay out the gardens at Ascott but was only concerned with the buildings, However, a general layout plan for the Ascott garden survives among the Devey office drawings at the Royal Institute of British Architects, and it is likely that he had some influence on the evolution of the gardens.

Unlike many architects, Devey was very interested in garden design and played a significant role in the revival of 'Old English' formal gardening, most notably through his restoration of the ancient layout at Penshurst Place in Kent. His architectural work in the garden at Ascott included the Tea House at the east end of the Madeira Walk, the Skating Hut overlooking the Lily Pond to the north of the house, and various 'Chinese Chippendale' garden seats. These all demonstrate the qualities adumbrated by Walter Godfrey in *Gardens in the Making* (1914). Godfrey recommended 'trellis of interlacing or jointed bars, from its long association with garden architecture' for the backs of seats, and advised against 'extremes of too

great a finish or too obvious a "rusticity"'. 'Make the outline simple and the details good', he wrote; 'the architects of the time of James I possessed perhaps the greatest felicity in this kind of design.' Devey, too, may have been responsible for suggesting the extensive use of topiary in the garden, which contemporaries found eccentric. *Country Life* in 1900 wrote of 'quaintly-clipped yews cut into shapes that those who revile topiary work consider a form of shrub slaughter'.

The main part of the garden at Ascott seems to have been laid out in the 1880s, following Leopold de Rothschild's marriage, and was conceived partly as a present for his wife and a celebration of their happy marriage. This explains details such as the motto round the sundial ('Light and shade by turn, but love always'). Further embellishment of the garden continued into the 1890s, the Jubilee Plantation at the south-east corner being planted in 1897, the rock garden grotto constructed in 1896 and, the most spectacular features of all, two fountains by Thomas Waldo Story erected in 1891.

Thomas Waldo Story was the son of the Rome-based American dilettante sculptor William Whetmore Story (1819–95), whose statue of *Cleopatra* was immortalised in Nathaniel Hawthorne's *The Marble Faun* (1860) and whose studio in the Palazzo Barberini was the centre of American expatriate cultural life in Italy. Thomas Waldo Story was educated in England – at Eton and Oxford – before he too followed in his father's footsteps and established a studio in Rome, in the Via San Martino.

In a 1903 article for *The Magazine of Art*, the art critic, E. March Phillipps, wrote about Thomas Waldo Story: 'When we find a sculptor who is at once inventive, prolific, original, and dignified, who uses his art as the Old Masters did, with the industry and practical adaptation of the craftsman who can turn his hand from one medium to another, and does not hesitate to give rein to

the love of decoration, we recognise that about such a man there is something large and refreshing. His art has a character and a reality of its own.'

March Phillipps continued: 'It was … *The Fallen Angel*, exhibited in 1887, that first gained him serious attention. The angel, with wing turned and broken under her, lies upon the ground, and an earthly youth is bending over her, bewildered by the exquisite vision. In some degree the pair recall the *Cupid and Psyshe* of Canova. The delicacy and purity of these two young nude figures, so entirely poetic in character, won unqualified praise for the young sculptor.' *The Fallen Angel* was recently acquired by Sir Evelyn and Lady de Rothschild for their London residence.

The fountains at Ascott are the first, and perhaps the best, of a series of exuberant bronze and marble fountains created by Story for some of Britain's most important houses. About the Venus Fountain, March Phillipps noted: 'The nude figure … is borne upon the back of a tortoise, placed in the middle of a gigantic sea shell. Two sea-horses are attached to the shell, and, rearing and plunging, have broken their reins, which remain in the grasp of a young Triton. Perched on the brim of the shell behind, a group of fairies, with whips in hand, joyously urge the speed of the sea monsters. The water squirts from the mouths of the horses, but the main volume comes out from under the tortoise and rushes through channels formed by the ribs of the shell, making a beautiful oval cascade. The group is placed in an immense

circular reservoir. The figures are of dark bronze, the dolphins of green bronze, and the basin of yellow Siena marble. The whole impression is of daring and exuberance. A joyous, dashing cadence reminds one that its creator has lived close to the famous fount of Trevi; indeed, of this, as of other work of Mr. Story's, we feel that without Bernini they would never have existed.' This fountain by Story set a fashion and was followed by similar work at Blenheim in Oxfordshire, for the Duke of Marlborough, and at Cliveden for the Astors. All combine extraordinary virtuosity in the modelling, carving and casting with successful overall design.

To the east of the Venus Fountain is the only piece of contemporary art in the Ascott collection. It is a major work by British artist Richard Long, called 'Ascott Circle'. Long (born Bristol, 1945) is internationally acknowledged as a key figure in the development of post-war art. Since the mid-1960s Long has taken a radical approach to nature and expanded the potential scale of art through the medium of walking in the landscape. Long's wilderness and rural walks, which articulate different ideas about time, measurement, space or material relationships, are presented using photographs and text. Some walks are also marked by sculptures made along the way. In addition Long has made sculptures in galleries and public spaces using mud, sticks and stones. In Long's formulation his photographs, texts and books engage the mind, while his sculptures engage the senses.

Regarding 'Ascott Circle', Graham Southern of

far left
'Ascott Circle' by
Richard Long

left
Lynn Garden, designed
by Jacques and Peter
Wirtz

Christie's wrote in July 2005: 'The work that Richard is proposing to make for you at Ascott House is without question one of the most important private commissions he has ever undertaken. He initially conceived this work for the G8 Summit and it was to be positioned directly in front of Gleneagles. Due to adverse developments this commission did not go ahead, however Richard is completely devoted to making it as he feels it would be in his words, "a classic Richard Long" and also a substantial new development in his work.' In unveiling the work in June 2006, Long explained the work with the following words:

A circle is real and symbolic.
A stone is real and symbolic.
Raw material: the land is made of stone(s) or parts thereof.
Cosmic variety: every stone is different, like fingerprints or snowflakes.
A circle of stones: from simplicity to complexity.

In a letter to Sir Evelyn and Lady de Rothschild in 2005 from Sardinia, Long said: 'The stone in this work is slate from Delabole in Cornwall, a source I have used for thirty years. Being sedimentary the slate splits naturally into thin pieces, so it is practical – I can manhandle and place each slate. Since 1972 I have made stone circles in different landscapes around the world – the Andes, Ireland, Iceland, Himalayas, Morocco, Scotland, Turkey, Mongolia, the Sahara, Sierra Nevada, Spitzburgen, Greece and Spain – different places connected by movement and a common idea.'

To the north of the house, directly to the west of the Serpentine Walk, which leads from the house to the Lily Pond, lies the Lynn Garden. In 2005, Sir Evelyn de Rothschild commissioned Jacques and Peter Wirtz to design this garden as a celebration of his marriage to Lynn Forester in 2000. The father-and-son team of garden designers is one of the most famous of the twentieth century, having designed the new gardens at the Tuilleries and also the gardens at Alnwick Castle in Northumberland. In conceiving of the Lynn Garden, Peter Wirtz wrote:

'The Lynn Garden at Ascott consists of variations on the old garden theme of the circle. Rarely in landscape architecture is one geometric form treated as an abstract idea and explored through a great number of transformations, concentrated in one garden.

At Ascott we found a unique challenge and opportunity to test this idea, contained in a framework of static yew hedges. It was not only an ideally secluded harbour to introduce a piece of modern landscape architecture to Ascott, but also very well suited to being challenged by a contrasting composition. A composition of circles disposed in a manner to provoke a great sense of dynamism. The compact density and the swirling movement almost seem to be trying to escape from their framework, in total denial of its dominance.

The different identities the circles take, from melancholic meditation to a playful spiral to a mysterious island or a full moonscape that rises out of a fur collar of grasses, allow the visitor to reflect on the endless

ways in which circular gardens can interact with the
pedestrian. Going around, going up, trying to get in and
out, trying to find the centre: the garden elements
manipulate the pedestrians by their own forces, and it is
no longer the pedestrians who dominate the garden!'

When inaugurating the garden in June 2006, Sir
Evelyn created a plaque, currently placed in the south
end of the Lynn Garden, which reads: 'Lynn, Life and
Love. A Garden for All.'

To the north of the Lynn Garden is the Lily Pond.
This was originally constructed by Leopold de Rothschild
to allow his wife, Marie, to ice skate in winter. The small
thatched cottage was designed by George Devey and is
where hot chocolate was served to skaters in winter. The
pond has recently been opened up, with a path running
around it.

The immediate landscape beyond the gardens was
planted with clumps of trees to create a park landscape
covering a further 300 acres. As at Waddesdon Manor,
much use was made of well-grown trees, including
many horse chestnuts, transported from the surrounding countryside under the direction of Mr Jennings. Two curving approach drives leading to the house
were laid, each with an entrance lodge designed by
Devey.

At the time he was laying out the gardens in the
1880s, Leopold was also expanding the estate. In 1885 he
spent £32,000 on buying additional land, and in 1889 he
bought Ascott Farm for £22,819. In addition to devel-
oping the South Court Stud, he laid out a three and a half
mile golf course and a cricket ground. The latter survives, with its pavilion, to the north-east of the house
behind the new hunting stables. It is surrounded by
trees and is among the most attractive private grounds
in England where regular matches are played in

summer. It is one of a group of similar cricket fields,
which include those at Arundel Castle in West Sussex
and Torry Hill in Kent, where the late Victorian tradition
of country-house cricket continues to flourish.

Leopold and Marie de Rothschild continued to
improve and alter the garden throughout their lives. In
1911, for instance, when the conservatory was demolished
to make way for the new drawing room at the west end
of the house, Walter Godfrey redesigned the immediate
layout to create a formal garden there with low-clipped
yew hedges and planting troughs. When the house itself
was sweepingly remodelled in 1937–8, most of the garden
was left as created in the nineteenth century apart from
some simplification of the planting. Over the years the
more elaborate Victorian bedding-out has been reduced
and some of the topiary removed, as well as many flowering trees and new planting being added to the garden.

TOUR OF THE GARDEN

The visitor to Ascott approaches the house from the main lodge on the Wing–Leighton Buzzard road. A curving drive leads through the area known as the north lawn, a large expanse of mown grass dotted with specimen trees including several fine oaks, cedars and large horse chestnuts.

The main part of the garden at Ascott lies to the south of the house, on gently sloping ground. There is a splendid prospect over the Vale of Aylesbury, with the Mentmore woods in the middle distance and the Chilterns closing the view to the south-east. It is a very English scene, with its hedged fields and soft outline, and it is still as completely rural-seeming as it was in the late nineteenth century, when the garden was first developed. In front of the house wide lawns and grass banks form a series of naturalistic terraces. Like the north lawn, these are scattered with a great variety of ornamental trees, including a good *Acer griseum*, Scarlet Oaks and Copper Beeches. The mulberry is thought to be a survivor from the original farmhouse garden. Seemingly random-placed pieces of topiary 'like daleks' hint at the surprise formal features that lie partly concealed by the fall in the ground to the south.

It is best to walk round the garden in a clockwise direction; in this way all the key features can be encountered in a logical sequence. From the Scented Walk on the east side of the house flights of steps bounded by beds of neatly clipped ivy and punctuated by ornamental vases, including replicas of Victorian Coade-stone pots, lead to the former Fern Garden, which is now known as the Sunken Garden. Here an exceptionally fine *Parrotia persica* can be admired in early spring, when the flowers, consisting of small tufts of crimson anthers, appear, and again in autumn, when its leaves assume rich red and gold tints.

Immediately to the south of the Sunken Garden is the giant evergreen sundial, possibly the most unusual garden feature at Ascott. It is composed entirely of clipped yew and box. The central gnomon, or style, is formed from two different varieties of yew grafted on to each other, with a golden ball on top and dark Irish yew below making it look like an egg in a cup. The dial is made up of large Roman numerals in clipped dwarf golden box, while the encircling motto – 'Light and shade by turn, but love always' – is of Golden Yew and has a heart at either end, also clipped in Golden Yew. There is an alternative route to the sundial via the Holly Border, a continuation of the Scented Walk containing a

collection of variegated hollies; it also goes past a bed of white- and yellow-flowering rhododendrons.

Stretching to the west from here is the Madeira Walk, a straight gravel path 100 yards long flanked by sheltered double borders. On the north side is a sunny brick wall, against which grow various kinds of ceanothus, old roses and aquilegias, phlox, campanulas and delphiniums, recently replanted in shades of mauve, lilac and blue. Along the top of this wall is a clipped hedge of Golden Holly, while backing the opposite bed is a magnificent hedge of Golden Yew. The top of the yew hedge is diversified with clipped topiary balls and mushrooms. Looking down the length of the Madeira Walk from the east end is the Tea House, designed by Devey and lined with Rust's Vitreous Mosaic in a bright turquoise shade.

left
The south front and terrace

above
Viburnum carlesii grows on the Scented Walk

above right
The evergreen sundial and its surrounding motto

Halfway down the Madeira Walk is the Venus Garden. This is a large circular enclosure surrounded by a yew hedge and containing a formal basin of water in which is sited Thomas Waldo Story's bravura Venus Fountain. East of the fountain is 'Ascott Circle', by Richard Long, made of split Delabole slate and installed in 2005.

Continuing westward, an area of 'well-groomed informality' is traversed. Cedars and more topiary are established across the lower lawns. Further over are a pair of Swamp cypresses and the Magnolia Dell, where the existing collection of magnolias has recently been enlarged. In the south-west corner of the garden is the Jubilee Plantation, an arboretum planted to commemorate Queen Victoria's Diamond Jubilee in 1897, which includes a Manna Ash, Paper Birch and Cut-leaf Beech. In spring the grass hereabouts is colourful, with thousands of naturalised daffodils.

Beyond the Jubliee trees will be found the Anne Avenue, which was planted by Sir Evelyn in memory of his sister, Anne. This leads on to the Chinese Dell, which is underplanted with 10,000 naturalised tulips of many colours. Returning to the gravel path and turning north, one encounters the Dutch Garden. This is the third of the major Victorian formal features at Ascott. A long enclosure

top
Madeira Walk

above
Cedrns atlantica grows on the lower lawn

surrounded by shrubby banks and clipped hedges contains neat little formal beds, which perpetuate the Victorian bedding-out, with different colour schemes in spring and summer. A particular feature are the *Coleus* hybrids, which were immensely popular with Victorian gardeners. The whole is overlooked by the second and more elegant of Story's fountains; this one is topped by a bronze statue of Eros. At the north end are the grotto and rockery, constructed of tufa blocks in 1896. This gives a good elevated view back over the formal pattern of the flower beds. The yew hedges are clipped to form a wave-like pattern. The path around the top of the Dutch Garden is lined with *Cornus kousa* and is thus known as the Cornus Walk.

Returning north towards the house, the visitor reaches the dell on the west side of the garden. This marks the site of the former orchard and retains some of its old character, with flowering fruit trees and ornamental cherries. The main path that runs below the house, with commanding views of the Vale of Aylesbury and the Dunstable Downs beyond, leads towards a clipped yew hedge and seat, and connects with paths returning to the Scented Walk.

Across the drive from the top of the Scented Walk, the north forecourt has been restored with a white marble fountain in the middle surrounded by eight clipped standard Portuguese laurels. On the central axis, the Long Walk has been reconstructed as a Serpentine Walk with new beech hedging in a traditional pattern. Half-way down is the Lynn Garden, by Jacques and Peter Wirtz. With two circular water features and several large planted mounds, it is a modern twist on the traditional arboretum.

At the end of the Serpentine Walk, the Lily Pond has long been one of Ascott's more famous features. It is a large oval expanse of water completely covered with water-lilies in the summer. It was also designed to serve as a skating pond in the winter. The Skating Hut, a picturesque thatched timber structure designed by George Devey, still stands on the south side. From here steps lead back to the north lawn and main drive.

above
The Dutch Garden with
Thomas Waldo Story's
Eros Fountain in its centre